# Ukraine in the Crosshairs

The Crisis of 2014 and Putin's
Surprising Role

By William Dunkerley

ⓟ Omnicom Press

Published by
Omnicom Press
New Britain, CT, USA
*Publishers since 1981*

www.OmnicomPress.com


Library of Congress Control Number: 2014953708
ISBN-10:0990452905
ISBN-13:978-0-9904529-0-4
Printed in the United States of America

*This book is dedicated to all the people of Ukraine. May they shed the affliction of foreign interventions and find unity and peace amongst themselves.*

# Preface

The year 2014 saw a dire crisis erupt in Ukraine. The trouble actually had its genesis in November 2013. At first there was a seemingly simple street protest lashing out against governmental corruption and seeking improved living standards.

But this turned out to be no single day event. Demonstrators camped out in the center of Ukraine's capital earnestly demanding change. Things picked up steam and within a couple of months they morphed into a full-blown revolution.

By early 2014 the revolutionaries ultimately threw out the president and the constitution and took charge of most of the country. Then, since not everyone supported the revolutionaries, a bloody civil war broke out in some areas.

My purpose in writing this book is not to chronicle all that led to civil war. The conflict is ongoing as I am writing. So it is also not my purpose to describe the current events in that counter-rebellion.

Instead, I'd like to tell you about something surprising that I discovered as I was following all the developments. What I found is that much of the storyline that we've all seen in the press is not supported by any facts. Indeed, it is a narrative that under close scrutiny actually seems intended to create a false impression of what the crisis is all about.

That's what this book is all about. It's not intended to document what has actually happened in Ukraine. But it will expose something about those who have tried to tell that story: They have done so through fabrications instead of facts.

Who or what could be behind such an extensive effort to deceive? Frankly, I don't know for sure. I'm not a conspiracy theorist at heart. I'm not writing here to convince you of any particular grand scheme that is being played out in the unfolding crisis.

What I will attempt, however, is to describe for you representative news stories and U.S. governmental positions that seem at variance with readily verifiable facts. In this way, you'll be able to grasp the surprising backstory, the story behind the story.

I'll supply enough background on related issues so you can appreciate the inconsistencies in all the public reports yourself. In doing so I refer to statistics, discuss history, and cite case examples. I don't represent this information to be definitive or exhaustive. It is provided simply in a belief that from it the reader will get a fair perspective with which to consider the reliability of the media and governmental accounts of the Ukrainian crisis. Those seeking greater definitiveness on the supporting issues should extend their research beyond this book.

There is also controversy over reliability issues in Ukrainian and Russian media reports and with information emanating from the governments of those countries. That controversy is outside the scope of this book, and I have not dealt with it here in detail. As such, I imply no comparison favorable or unfavorable between the U.S.

coverage and that of the other countries.

And finally, in Chapter 10 I'll offer several hypotheses I've heard that might explain why deception could be afoot here. These are not theories that I am urging you to believe. They are simply offered to be thought provoking. Meanwhile we all await concrete evidence of why fabrications instead of the truth were put forth to describe the Ukrainian crisis of 2014.

Just a note on terminology: Much of the reportage on the crisis couches it as a conflict between regions. Thus I make frequent use of the terms East, West, South, and Eastern and Western. In all cases, I am referring to regions of Ukraine. One exception is my use of the term Western media or Western press. In these cases, I am referring to the media in the United States and Western Europe.

W.D.
November 2014

# Contents

# Chapter 1
# In Whose Crosshairs?

*It seems that multiple foreign and domestic actors have taken aim.*

**PUTIN** has set his steely sights on Ukraine. That's been the unbending belief of President Barack Obama. He emphatically accused Russia of "seeking through force to exert influence on a neighboring country."

Obama was talking, of course, about the violent 2014 crisis, ongoing as this is being written. It started with earnest street demonstrations and grew into a bloody revolution. It led to protest leaders taking over in Kyiv, the capital, and Russia assuming control of the Crimean peninsula in the south, and finally to civil war in the East.

The Obama administration also claims that in July 2014 Russia had Malaysia Airlines Flight 17 in its crosshairs when the jetliner was shot out of the Ukrainian sky killing nearly 300 people. The plane may have been mistaken for a Ukrainian military transport. But it was Russia that supplied the advanced weaponry and expertise, according to the administration.

Russian president Vladimir Putin rejected Obama's condemnatory claims all around. He asserted it was Obama who had Ukraine in the crosshairs. Putin glibly said the political crisis started as "a state coup supported by our U.S. and European partners." He believes they're the culprits who created the mess in the first place. The airplane disaster was just another consequence of America's meddling.

Amidst those opposing views, one thing is clear: This high-stakes drama has pitted the United States against the Russian Federation in a confrontation that noted historian Stephen F. Cohen believes is the worst since the 1962 Cuban missile crisis.

## The Plight of Ukrainians

While the U.S. and Russia exchange accusations about who's to blame for the Ukrainian crisis, the predicament of the Ukrainian people seems to be lost in the shuffle.

News reports tend to focus on the hyperbolic rhetoric that is being tossed back and forth between the American and Russian sides. It's true that each side has its own cadre of groupies within the Ukrainian population. But what about the main body of Ukrainians? Where are they left in all this?

Ukraine is one of the most impoverished countries in Europe. An International Monetary Fund report for 2013 ranks it fourth from the bottom of all Europe. Its per-capita GDP is less than one tenth that of France's. According to *Forbes* magazine, "Ukraine is still struggling to recover from the 2008-2009 economic crisis while seeing its debt ($15.3 billion) skyrocket, among other financial woes."

The country is second largest in Europe in land area (European Russia is the largest), and eighth in terms of population. It is a country with great potential. But, according to Transparency International, it is the most corrupt country in all of Europe.

Ukraine is on its sixth president since the country's founding in 1991. Revolutions ushered two of them into power. And in each revolution there is convincing evidence that foreign interests took advantage of the Ukrainians. The foreigners exploited for their own questionable ends the Ukrainian passion for finding a government that can

lead the citizens to a better way of life.
If we view the Ukrainians seeking to better themselves as the hero-protagonists of this saga, then the foreign actors that have exploited Ukraine's tragic plight are decidedly the villains. The villains' victim is Ukraine itself.

Before the tug-of-war between the U.S. and the EU on one side, and Russia on the other, Ukraine existed with intact borders and without the tragedy of civil war.

### In the Current Crisis...

For now, Obama blames Putin for Ukraine's troubles, and Putin blames Obama. As you'll see in this book there are clear indications of some sort of foreign complicity. It is a contentious issue.

Exactly where the truth lies in all this may surprise you. Is it on the side of the U.S., or does Russia have it right?

Many media reports paint the situation as if the choice is really that simple, one or the other. But it isn't. Putin and Obama are not the only ones that have Ukraine in the crosshairs.

The world media has also had the country in its sights since late November 2013. The general storyline has been that a democracy-seeking Ukraine is also seeking integration into Europe and escape from domination by Vladimir Putin's oppressive Russia. Ukrainians rose up to fight for their freedom. Mass demonstrations cropped up across much of the country, voicing demands for change.

The main protest venue was Kyiv's central square, popularly called Maidan, and the protest movement took on that name as its moniker.

On Maidan, protestors were loudly condemning the alleged massive corruption in the government of President Victor Yanukovych, as well as his decision to abandon the pursuit of an association and trade agreement with the European Union.

The *Kyiv Post* reported, "Kyivans take to streets on November 21 to protest government's decision to drop EU deal." The next day, the U.S. Department of State announced that Secretary John Kerry was dropping plans for his trip to Ukraine scheduled for early December.

As the protests grew over time, the crowd erected tents, built fires that flamed high into the night skies, occupied government buildings, and rioted. There were clashes with the police and reports of protesters sustaining serious injuries. But the protests continued undaunted.

Things got a lot worse on February 20, 2014 when sniper fire rang out from atop buildings, killing many protestors and some police. The government was widely considered responsible for the sniper killings.

Four days later, Yanukovych fled Kyiv contending that threats had been made against his life. Protestors seized that opportunity to take control of the capital, establish their own government, and throw out the extant constitution. It was a breakdown of constitutional order. What had started as a mass protest was now effectively a revolution that succeeded in taking over most of the country and installing an interim junta.

The revolutionary leaders promised democratic elections in the near future, and indeed they occurred on May 25, installing business tycoon Petro Poroshenko as the new president.

## The Foreign Agitators

Make no mistake, though, Maidan had been no straight-forward people-against-government altercation. I've seen a plethora of other active players both within and outside Ukraine.

For instance, the European Union, surprisingly, is alleged to have Ukraine in its sights.

That was confirmed by U.S. State Department official Victoria Nuland in her profanity-laced telephone comments to America's ambassador to Kyiv. She notoriously suggested that the U.S. circumvent EU participation in America's initiative to remake the political power structure in Ukraine.

So not only has the EU been involved, but the U.S. was unhappy about it.

Nuland's phone call also reveals, of course, that the U.S. has its own agenda for Ukraine. Ukraine is in America's crosshairs, too.

According to independent international affairs analyst Patrick Armstrong: "It has been revealed that the EU spent 496 million Euros subsidizing front groups in Ukraine between 2004 and 2013. Then we have Victoria Nuland reporting the U.S. has spent $5 billion on Ukraine. Brussels and Washington have lit the fuse, the fire is burning. It was easy to start; but will be hard to finish."

Why have America and the EU been in there reshaping Ukraine in the first place? That's a good question, and I'll dig into that in subsequent chapters.

But it has been Russia's focus on Ukraine that garnered the greatest news coverage. I've seen many news stories that claim Putin is out to either take over Ukraine, or destabilize and divide it.

Putin plays a very dark role here. After all, Crimea, once part of Ukraine, has now become part of Russia. Almost everyone believes that was Putin's doing. Indeed, the fact Crimea is now Russian territory seems to speak for itself.

Even so, there are two sides to the story. Side

one says that Crimea was invaded and annexed. Side two claims what happened was merely a democratically-driven Crimean reunification with Russia from whence it came years back.

Each side thinks the other's explanation is utterly ridiculous. But I can't help thinking that neither side is articulating a very cogent position. Their back-and-forth bickering ignores the underlying plight of the Ukrainian people.

## The Internal Groupies

Each foreign side in this dispute has its own advocates within Ukraine.

Side one is primarily made up by the various factions in Western Ukraine. They're the revolutionaries who have taken control in Kyiv. Their leaders exhibit a gut-level antipathy toward Russia in public statements. Their spokespeople express a desire for a closer relationship with the EU and for distancing Ukraine from Russia.

The second side is in Eastern Ukraine. Activists there are popularly called separatists, sometimes even terrorists. Their spokespeople deny the legitimacy of the revolution, and express favor for cooperative coexistence with Russia. It's said they want out of Ukraine. But after declaring their own republic, they were attacked by Kyiv-led forces. Civil war has broken out between the Kyiv regime and the Easterners. Where this will go is a confusing issue as this book is being written.

In recent years Ukrainian central leadership has been electorally passed back and forth between these two sides like a football. The result has satisfied nobody. Neither population wants to be dominated by the other. This fundamental internal conflict has been a powerful force in propelling the Maidan movement as well as eliciting the negative reactions of its opponents.

The Western Ukrainian activists think the leadership of the Russian speakers in the East is illegitimate and under the control or influence of Moscow. The Easterners, on the other hand, believe that the junta in Kyiv is illegitimate. Their disagreement has become bloody, and many have died, Ukrainians fighting Ukrainians.

Controversy exists over the status of non-

Ukrainians who have fought along side of the Easterners. Some maintain that they are foreign mercenaries or volunteers. The U.S. contends they were sent by Moscow. But as you'll see in subsequent chapters, attempts to substantiate that contention have relied upon fabrications.

There was a third side, Crimea, with its widely-reported Russian-speaking majority. It was content to be in Ukraine before the Maidan takeover, but was spooked by the fall of the democratic government. It subsequently voted to reunify with Russia, and thus is no longer part of the Ukrainian picture.

**A Complex Problem**

Of course, the East-West dilemma has more to it than the simple linguistic and geographical differences that dominate the news. In the next chapter you'll see what a complex lingua-ethnic imbroglio this is.

But notice all the different sides in what has become an abject tragedy in Ukraine. There's the Eastern Ukrainians, the Western Ukrainians, both with their respective subgroups. Then there's the United States, the European Union, and Russia. They all have Ukraine in their crosshairs.

Doesn't this sound like Ukraine is getting it from all sides?

Being in someone's crosshairs is an uncomfortable place to be. It means someone's got it in for you.

Frankly, I wonder if any of those players have at heart the welfare of Ukraine and its citizens. It sure seems like Ukraine is being tugged back and forth by insiders and outsiders in the pursuit of their self-serving agendas.

Pity the poor populace at large.

## Cast of Characters

This crosshairs drama has several key individual players in the media reports. The central character is not even a Ukrainian. It is Vladimir Putin, president of Russia. He is cast as the villain.

Next is Victor Yanukovych. He is the corrupt, Russia-leaning politician who was thrown out by the democracy-seeking protesters.

The new guard consisted initially of Arseniy Yatsenyuk, the new prime minister, and interim president Olexander Turchynov. Then in May came Petro Poroshenko, the newly elected president.

Each player seems to have his own version of the facts on what's going on in Ukraine.

But where does the truth lie amid so many conflicting accounts? Obviously, a lot depends upon the observer's perspective and biases.

In subsequent chapters, we'll analyze the reliability of media and governmental information since the start of Maidan, sort through the various claims and renditions of the "truth," and get to the bottom of this all.

# Chapter 2
# Ukraine's Lingua-Ethnic Dilemma

*Are political agitators stirring the pot?*

**MANY** news stories on the Ukrainian crisis allege a rift between the Russian speakers in the East and South and the Ukrainian speakers in the West. For instance, Sergei Markov, a political analyst in Moscow, writing in the *Moscow Times*, contends "at the heart of the conflict is a deep division between the Ukrainian-speaking and Russian-speaking populations."

Is Markov on to something here? If he is, that's quite a dilemma. Is it the source of the trouble?

Not everyone sees language as *the* divisive factor. CNN interviewed a Russian-speaking photojournalist who lives in Kyiv. She explained, "My kids speak Ukrainian in school and with many of their friends, and we speak Russian at home. When my son's fourth-grade teacher talks to me, she speaks Ukrainian. I respond in Russian. We don't even notice that our conversation is in two languages."

## The Kyiv Compromise?

Fred Weir, correspondent for the *Christian Science Monitor*, says this kind of cross-language exchange is called the "Kyiv Compromise." He explains:

"Two people meet and one begins talking in his or her preferred language -- say, Ukrainian. The other responds in Russian, and the conversation takes off, going back and forth, seemingly without missing a beat. If you didn't listen closely, you might never guess that there are two distinctly different languages in play.

"That compromise, as a stroll down any Kyiv avenue will confirm, is a mundane reality. It holds true across large swaths of central Ukraine. Head west and Ukrainian gradually becomes the only language you hear. To the east or south, it's Russian that heavily dominates. Ask any Kyivan what he or she thinks about it and you're liable to get a live-and-let-live sort of shrug, with the answer that they really don't think about it much at all. It's just part of getting along."

That's Kyiv and central Ukraine. But what about the rest of the country? The CNN interviewee mentioned above shared an observation on that. She pointed out that even in the western city of Lviv, where Ukrainian predominates, language was not a problem for her. "I never had anybody look down on me for my Russian," she exclaimed.

## The Politics of Language

In contrast to these reports of friendly accommodation between Ukrainian and Russian language speakers, the constitution designates Ukrainian as the sole state language nationwide. Russian and other languages may be used freely in social life. And in recent years Russian has been allowed as a second official language in some areas.

That's a point of contention, however. Writing in *Ukrainian Week* for May 21, 2014, journalist Oleksandr Kramar claims, "If Russian becomes the second state language or even acquires official status in part of Ukraine's territory, this will aggravate the discrimination of the Ukrainian-speaking majority."

But where is this "discrimination of the Ukrainian-speaking majority" that Kramar talks about? There's not much evidence of it. (See Appendix II.)

Many believe that given the ubiquity of Russian, that it too should be approved for use as a second official language nationally.

It is puzzling that amidst the stories told by CNN and in the *Christian Science Monitor* of peaceful linguistic coexistence, language is a hot political issue in Ukraine.

One of the revolutionary parliament's first acts was a vote to repeal the law that permitted Russian to be used regionally as an official language in areas having a significant Russian-speaking population. After some time and a lot of pressure, the interim president ended up not signing that legislation into law. That may have been too late to avoid triggering fears among Russian speakers that their language and culture were in danger of becoming subsumed by a future mandate to use Ukrainian exclusively. It's a fear of what the Western Ukrainians who now control Kyiv might do to the Russian speakers in the future.

So the flip side of Ukrainian speakers' fear of being permissive about the use of Russian is the Russian speakers' apprehension that enforced use of Ukrainian might stifle the free use of Russian.

The result seems to be that fear arises within both language groups that their respective language and culture may get short-changed.

There is another argument offered by some Ukrainian speakers. They feel that during Soviet times Ukrainian was officially repressed and now deserves state support. There is also a sense that Ukraine deserves its own state language unambiguously.

**The Impact of Language Politics**

Some observers assert that the revolutionary parliament's knee-jerk action against the use of Russian is what precipitated the Crimean vote to secede from Ukraine and reunify the region with Russia.

There has been a lot of political rhetoric and high emotions about language matters.

The language issue remains a sticking point.

## Whence Language Discrimination?

Professor Nicolai Petro of the University of Rhode Island offers some historical background on the languages of Ukraine: "Under Peter the Great, the Russian government began to encourage literacy and education, which was understood as instilling a standardized form of Russian, and suppressing various 'local dialects.'" That must have been quite a boon to Empire-wide governance and commerce. The utility would have been greatly appreciated in cities -- centers of government and business -- but less relevant in the countryside.

So it comports, as Petro adds, that "after the union between Russia and Ukraine in the mid-17th century, Russian gradually became dominant in cities, while Ukrainian was more widely spoken in rural areas."

Perhaps that's why some present day Russians think of Ukrainian as simply a peasant dialect, a corrupted form of Russian, a hillbilly Russian so to speak. But to the contrary Petro explains, "By most accounts the Ukrainian language developed more or less simultaneously alongside Russian and other Eastern Slavic languages, becoming distinct from the rest around the 14th century."

Petro further expounds that "by the early 19th century [the policy to standardize Russian] was so successful that even many educated Ukrainians regarded 'the Little Russian dialect,' as Ukrainian was then known, as a debased form of Russian." But, of course, it wasn't.

Nonetheless, Ukrainian still suffers in comparison to Russian in certain quarters. Some years ago there was a joke going around on that subject: "A group of Ukrainian parliamentarians were sitting together in an informal discussion. The conversation was in Ukrainian. At some point one of the ethnic Ukrainians notices that by then all the ethnic Russians had left for other appointments. He says to his colleagues, "Look, there are no 'Russian speakers' left, now we can start speaking in Russian."

Noted Ukrainian intellectual Mykola Ryabchuk once told an audience in Toronto that many people consider that Ukrainian has a low social status. It's been suggested that in Ukraine, many formal presentations are given in the Ukrainian language. But, said Ryabchuk, as soon as the microphones are turned off, conversation switches over to Russian.

I've seen reports that when former presidents Leonid Kravchuk and Leonid Kuchma travelled to Moscow on official business, they brought along translators to have the Russian of their interlocutors translated into Ukrainian. But, according to Ryabchuk, when they were at home with their families, the former presidents spoke Russian.

Political correctness seems to be another factor in the language issue.

## Language Misunderstandings

Fred Weir interviewed Lyudmilla Kudryavtseva, a professor of linguistics at Kyiv's Shevchenko University on the language issue. She told him, "My ancestors have lived on what is now Ukrainian territory since the 18th Century, and we've always been Russian speakers." She added, "When we voted for independence, no one told us we would be forced to change our age-old identity, to unlearn our native tongue, and speak a different language. That wasn't part of the original deal."

Her last statement may have been an exaggeration. No one was really forced to unlearn Russian. But the claimed fear of Kramar that the existence of Russian speech on Ukrainian soil would inevitably lead to discrimination against native Ukrainian speakers was likewise an exaggeration.

The situation in the Baltic countries regarding their Russian speakers has been quite different from what is unfolding in Ukraine: Russian lost its official language status following the end of the Soviet Union. And Russian speakers found themselves politically disenfranchised in the land of their birth. Yet after more than 20 years of those official policies, there have been no civil wars. Doesn't that lend credence to the notion that the Ukrainian crisis at its heart is not about compelling language differences?

**Deliberately Not Getting Along**

Another consideration was raised by one of Fred Weir's interviewees: Oleksiy Kolomiyets, president of the Center for

European and Transatlantic Studies in Kyiv. In 2010 he told Weir, "If Russian were an official language, the main fear is that it would be a wide-open door for Russian influence in Ukraine."

Well, since then there has been a period when Russian was officially a second language in certain regions. Did that lead to Moscow calling the shots in those regions in the pre-Maidan era? No it didn't. The hypothesis has been disproved. But that 2010 fear expressed by Kolomiyets sounds an awful lot like the 2014 fear of Kramar.

Why is the misunderstanding persisting despite evidence that it is not reality based? Isn't this a case of deliberately not getting along? What's with this?

A sentiment cited by Weir hits the nail on the head, I think. Referencing Kolomiyets' statement about his own personal fears, Weir observed that "others say if the politicians would not stir the pot, Ukrainians could live with the Kyiv Compromise."

That suggests the crisis is a product of rabble-rousing politicians, not language differences. Is that the answer?

Before we jump to that conclusion, let's consider one other possible explanation. Some allege that the root of the divisiveness in Ukraine is ethnic in nature. Is that it?

## Is Ethnicity the Culprit?

What about ethnicity? Are there forces trying to establish an ethnic state on soil where there is now a multiethnic mix? Is this crisis rooted in ethnicity?

Petro cites the latest official census as showing that "78 percent of Ukrainians identify themselves ethnically as Ukrainian, while only 17 percent call themselves ethnically Russian." That leaves 5 percent of "others." He also points out that by the time the Soviet Union ended in 1991, "the population was widely intermixed, with some 20 percent of families being mixed marriages between Russians and Ukrainians."

There's something this finding doesn't touch upon, however. It's the question of how many of the Russians and Ukrainians in non-mixed marriages were themselves the progeny of mixed marriages from earlier generations. The phenomena of mixed marriages did not originate at the time the Soviet Union ended. It goes back generations.

Both Kyiv and Moscow are using polarizing rhetoric about language and ethnicity to support their respective political positions. But they are being absolutist about things that are not really black and white. They are taking positions that defy reality and reason.

## So What's the Dilemma?

The reality seems to be that a number of ethnic Ukrainians have a good dose of Russian blood in them. And similarly many ethnic Russians are not free of Ukrainian DNA. So when people say they are ethnic Ukrainian or ethnic Russian, the distinction may be more social or political than genetic.

I see two bottom line conclusions here.

First, it seems to be that Ukraine is a country of considerable ethnic mixture. Statistics on the percentages of ethnic Ukrainians and ethnic Russian are unreliable. That's because the collection of census data hasn't allowed for counting people of mixed ethnicity. And with data suggesting a very significant number of mixed marriages over a protracted period of time, the so-called ethnic distinctions are in fact very indistinct. The tallies of how many citizens are ethnic Ukrainians and how many are ethnic Russians are unsupportable.

Second, it seems that Ukraine is really a bilingual country in which there is considerable political pressure to deny its bilinguality. Anecdotal evidence suggests that if left without political interference, the population can cope adequately with its bilinguality. But there is also evidence that segments of the population experience distress when they believe that the language and culture that they feel closest to is going to be contained or suppressed.

With that background, it is hard to understand the reasonableness behind Ukraine's declaration that it is officially monolingual. Why, even Israel is bilingual, with both Hebrew and Arabic being official languages.

So in Ukraine, while news reports and politicians talk about the Ukrainian dilemma being between Ukrainian and Russian language speakers, or between the two ethnicities, the reality seems elsewhere. You've seen here the way in which these factors are not nearly as differentiating when you look beneath the surface.

It seems to me that the conflict in Ukraine over languages is the product of citizens being manipulated by politicians, oligarchs, foreigners, etc. The language issue is just a tool in the manipulation.

A big shift toward opposing bilinguality occurred when discord and a parliamentary brawl broke out over a 2012 controversial language bill says Oleksiy Antypovych, principle of the Rating Group, a research firm. That was the bill that gave special status to Russian in regions with the highest number of Russian speakers.

Over the years various parties have used references to language and ethnicity to fuel discontent. By comparison, in America the ideal of social diversity and egalitarianism is largely a bedrock of society. But in Ukraine political forces seem to have turned that ideal into the negative concept of divisiveness.

There is some evidence that absent

provocation by politicians, the general population can largely manage to coexist in a united bilingual and multiethnic state. It is too early to know how this willingness to coexist will be impacted by the violent takeover in Kyiv and the bloody civil war in the East.

This all goes to show what the "Lingua-Ethnic Dilemma" is: It's whether to believe language and ethnicity are actually the divisive issues that the press and political agitators claim them to be, or to believe that they are not. (See more details on the lingua-ethnic issue in Appendix II.)

Here are the takeaway points from this chapter:

The trouble in Ukraine is not actually about language.

It's not about ethnicity.

It's about discord and malevolence and, yes, even civil war being instigated by parties who likely believe they have something to gain from it all. I'm talking about both foreign instigators and their local accomplices.

Later in this book I'll suggest who those parties might be.

## Chapter 3
# Fueling the Maidan Expectations

*Foreigners promote inflated hopes.*

**BACK** on December 15, 2013, Senator John McCain personally stirred the crowds on Maidan. He told them, "The free world is with you, America is with you, I am with you." As I watched news clips of McCain addressing the protestors, I wondered why a U.S. senator was doing that.

At issue was whether Ukraine would cast its lot with the EU or with Russia, according to McCain. The EU had put forth an association and trade agreement. Russian President Vladimir Putin in response had offered financial incentives to help Ukraine's sinking economy, including membership in a customs union with Russia, Belarus and Kazakhstan.

McCain impassionedly made this sound like a struggle between good and evil. Perhaps a fight between actual good and evil is enough to inspire a bloody revolution. But a trade and association agreement?

Not everyone agreed with McCain. French

politician Marine Le Pen went on record saying, "I think that there is no point for Ukraine to join the European Union." Her remark was carried in an interview by Voice of Russia. Readers of her comments responded very vociferously. They tended to believe that the EU is overplaying its hand in courting Ukraine. There was a general sense that the EU is now a troubled, overly bureaucratic organization with little to offer Ukraine.

Some suggested that the real issue is just an attempt to alienate Ukraine from Russia by any means. Is that what this is really about? What motive might lead foreigners to pursue such an objective?

**McCain's Warning**

McCain claims there's more to this than simply Ukraine's choice regarding the EU. He has told media organizations that President Putin is really seeking to reestablish the Russian Empire. McCain has long-opposed greater engagement with Russia, saying, "Moscow and Washington do not share common interests or values."

On some occasions McCain has accused

Putin of trying to bring back the old Soviet Union. But whether it's the Soviet Union or the Russian Empire, I've never seen where McCain has backed up his claims with any evidence at all. And without substantiation doesn't his rhetoric just amount to fear mongering?

Is this really just about whether Ukraine leans toward Russia or the EU? If so, it's hard to justify all the media fuss it's generated, much less the violent citizen emotions that have been inspired.

In the U.S. we've had polarized debates over North American trade agreements. But they didn't spiral out of control like the situation in Ukraine. Why has the result been so different in Ukraine?

Perhaps there is a hidden agenda somewhere in this Ukrainian crisis. There's been no transparency on who paid for all the organization and publicity for the demonstrations. Knowing who it was might be very informative.

Before all the McCain and other Western hoopla about the EU agreement, only 38 percent of Ukrainians supported the initiative. That was the finding of a poll sponsored by the British government. The study also showed that the country was widely split on this issue. In the Ukrainian-speaking West, support topped out at 70 percent. But in the largely Russian-speaking East, support was a paltry 12 percent.

Clearly McCain and his cohorts were playing with fire when they inflamed passions over this divisive issue.

## A Naive Sidekick

On McCain's junket to the Kyiv demonstrations he was accompanied by Connecticut's junior senator Chris Murphy. The two stood together on the Maidan stage to address the crowd. McCain a Republican and Murphy a Democrat seem to have an affinity when it comes to anti-Russia rhetoric.

For instance, in June 2013, while chairing a Senate hearing, Murphy likened justice in contemporary Russia to Stalin's Great Purge. He must not understand history very well to have said that.

Upon Murphy's return from Kyiv, he told

BBC, "It's in the U.S. interests for the Ukraine, as Ukraine citizens want, to orient itself towards Europe." When the BBC anchor challenged Murphy's assertion about what Ukrainians really prefer, he awkwardly responded, "I don't claim that it's a 95/5 proposition. But I think it's pretty clear that ... Ukraine wants to be part of Europe." Perhaps Murphy was unaware that earlier polls showed very mixed results on how much Ukrainians favor European integration.

Back in Murphy's home state, remarking on Murphy's Kyiv adventure, Paul Choiniere, opinion page editor of *The Day* wrote, "it is now clear he would have been better off staying home, or at least off that [Maidan] stage.

I've observed Murphy's frequent use of the term "the Ukraine." That's a touchy point in itself. Many Ukrainians prefer simply "Ukraine," believing that the former denigrates the country by suggesting it is merely a provincial region as in earlier times. The government has even taken an official position on the matter.

In 2009, just months after Barack Obama

was inaugurated as president, Radio Free Europe ran a story that belittled former vice-president Dick Cheney for calling the country "the Ukraine." I've seen no sign that the U.S. government sponsored broadcaster will now give Murphy the same treatment.

## Playing Ukrainians as Suckers

McCain told the Maidan crowd, "the destiny you seek lies in Europe." Murphy expanded on that, saying, "Ukraine's future stands with Europe, and the U.S. stands with Ukraine." Their remarks were made in the context of Ukraine's acquiring an extended relationship with the EU.

Doesn't that sound like they're telling Ukrainians that the EU is the solution to their enormous problems?

Vitali Klitschko, a Ukrainian politician, told *Foreign Policy* magazine, "We are a hardworking people who want to live as a modern European country. It's that simple."

But, oh, it's not. These people are misleading vulnerable Ukrainians to believe that the EU is a simple answer to their country's very serious problems. That's not to say that increasing ties with Western Europe is bad. But it's not the ultimate answer it's been made out to be.

I'm reluctant to call these guys snake oil salesmen, but the similarities are unmistakable. A snake oil salesperson is someone who plays upon a person's desperation for a cure to sell them a solution that is obviously fraudulent if critically examined.

Ukrainians were looking for a way of advancing their quality of life, and this is what they got.

Let's not forget that McCain, Murphy, and Klitschko are all politicians. Their empty statements seem more destined to generate votes and campaign contributions from their various constituencies than to address the consequences of a proposed solution.

**Not So Simple**

McCain and his cohorts all couch the situation as a choice Ukraine must make between Russia and the EU. That sentiment has been echoed in many media reports. For instance:

--"Ukrainians Face Choice between EU and Russia," NPR, December 2, 2013
--"Ukraine's Choice: East Or West?" Radio Free Europe, November 15, 2013
--"Russia and Europe Vie to Win the Prize of Ukraine," *Wall Street Journal*, November 15, 2013

Who imposed this choice? According to an article appearing in the *Telegraph*, "the EU gave Kiev a stark choice. Brussels told Ukraine that it cannot participate in several integration projects at the same time; it must make its choice."

Germany's Angela Merkel saw it differently. A *Kyiv Post* headline read, "Merkel: Ukraine should not be forced to choose between EU and Russia."

There are sound economic reasons why Ukraine should not be financially divorced from Russia. Both countries have been dependent upon each other as trading partners. According to the World Trade Organization, Russia has been Ukraine's largest trading partner. Ukraine has been Russia's third largest trading partner, reports Eurostat.

## A Way Out of the Hole?

The EU has put forth a "Support Package for Ukraine." But I haven't seen that it comes even close to compensating for the economic damage done to Ukraine by the U.S.- and EU-instigated rift between Russia and Ukraine.

The EU says its support package will "help the country's transition and boost the role of civil society, promoting and monitoring democratic reforms and inclusive socioeconomic development in Ukraine." Part of the program will "offer more opportunities for student mobility, academic cooperation, and youth exchanges."

It's hard to believe that the EU is proposing these kinds of feel-good initiatives in the current dire climate. The package does have more serious financial components. But I've seen no indication that that a careful analysis has been made of the still-unfolding economic damage vis-a-vis relations with Russia. Certainly that would have to be a first step before one could even understand the magnitude of a "Support Package" that would be needed.

## The Pre-Maidan Scene

Even before Maidan, the World Bank painted a dismal picture of Ukraine's predicament. In an October 7, 2013 "Economic Update" WB reported:

--Real GDP continued to decline in first half of 2013.
--In reaction to weak fiscal performance, the authorities adopted several worrisome measures.
--Foreign reserves of the National Bank of Ukraine declined to 2.4 months of imports at the beginning of October 2013.
--Macroeconomic imbalances are projected to widen further in 2013.
--Forecasts for 2014-2015 are dependent on domestic policy choices and external conditions.

Given these serious problems, how could a swing over to the EU possibly have looked like the piece of cake McCain and Murphy made it out to be. And Klitschko? "It's that simple?" What possibly could that guy have been thinking of?

## An IMF Bailout

The International Monetary Fund seems to be taking a more realistic and businesslike view of things. In April 2014 it announced a 2-year $17 billion program.

There are indications that IMF has at least an inkling of the size of the problem. But Al Jazeera reported: "The IMF has been wary about lending to Ukraine after two previous loan plans since 2008 failed because of the government's lack of adherence to reform conditions set by the global body. It has insisted on the reduction of huge fuel subsidies and improved efforts against widespread corruption in the government." AJ emphasized, "The loans are subject to IMF demands that Ukraine cuts subsidies for fuel, reduces its large deficit, controls pay rises, reduces corruption, and reforms its banking system."

Those are some very tall orders. Talk of jacking up everyone's energy costs and disallowing pay raises adds up to a major call for austerity. Back in 2010 Greece's call for austerity led to significant civil unrest. With the Ukrainian history of taking to the streets in protest, austerity will certainly be a challenging undertaking for the new government.

But perhaps even more daunting will be dealing with corruption.

## There's Corruption?

When asked how the corruption problem will be addressed, Reza Moghadam, director of the IMF's European Department explained, "Given long-standing challenges that have weakened Ukraine's economy, strengthening governance, enhancing transparency, and improving the business climate will be central elements of the program. Policy measures in these areas will include the adoption of a new procurement law to reduce exemptions from regular competitive procedures, measures to facilitate value-added tax refunds for businesses, and high-frequency audits of Naftogaz's accounts."

He used an awful lot of words to say not much. A new procurement law may be a nice touch, as will be more frequent audits. But Moghadam's plan amounts to trying to use a feather to knock over an elephant.

Transparency International gives Ukraine a corruption rating of 25. That's on a scale where a high number is good (i.e., freedom from corruption), and a low number is bad. Twenty five is a failing grade. It puts Ukraine's corruption on the same level as Nigeria's. Just to calibrate things, in Europe, Denmark leads the way with a rating of 91. Ukraine's corruption problem is worse than Russia's. Moghadam and the IMF need to get more serious about Ukraine's corruption.

## The Economic Bosses

A related problem is the domination of the economy by a select group of oligarchs, i.e., business tycoons and enterprising politicians who many claim play by their own rules. It doesn't seem that a new procurement law is going to address that problem.

According to the *Eurasia Daily Monitor*, in 2008 the wealthiest 50 Ukrainians had a net worth that equaled twice the country's annual state budget. Their wealth accounts for 85 percent of Ukraine's GDP. In Russia, a country notorious for a history of oligarchic abuse of the economy, its top 50 wealthiest represent only 35 percent of the country's GDP. If the *Eurasia Daily Monitor*'s facts are anywhere near correct, this is a seemingly insurmountable problem for Ukraine, and one for which the IMF seems to have only a featherweight understanding.

One last tidbit the *Eurasia Daily Monitor* pointed to: The greatest concentration of this elite wealth lies with members of the Party of Regions, a political party of which current president Petro Poroshenko was one of the founders. (Poroshenko now claims to be politically independent.) One-third of the wealthy elite's assets is held by members of the Party of Regions.

## Corruption in Education

An October 4, 2012 *Kyiv Post* article pulls no punches on the subject of corruption in education: "As everybody knows, the greatest problem in the Ukrainian education system is corruption. Students, or their parents, pay for entry into institutions of higher education, and if necessary, also for exams and degrees." This so-called "pay" is what most of us would call bribery.

The EU Support Package for Ukraine includes "opportunities for student mobility, academic cooperation, and youth exchanges." But it is silent about the problem of corruption in education.

Doesn't the EU know about it? Doesn't it sound like the EU has its assistance priorities wrong?"

The *Kyiv Post* article goes on, "If Ukraine is to catch up economically with the outside world, it needs good education. In many ways, Ukraine's education sector is its strongest part of the economy; but the best parts of the Ukrainian education system are dwindling remnants of the Soviet system, notably basic education in mathematics, and science."

I wonder if the IMF is thinking about this problem. It is IMF that is targeting corruption in Ukraine. But the central elements of its program seem to ignore the looming problem of corruption in education.

None of this inspires much hope for success of the IMF and EU interventions.

## McPromises

McCain's promises to the Ukrainian people of a brighter future with the EU now sound quite disingenuous. Surely he knows something about the country's tragic economic plight, doesn't he? And the oligarchic clamp on the economy? Is he oblivious to that? And what about the EU's and IMF's dumbed-down notion of how to fix things. That too.

While it is too early to judge what the new revolutionary regime can achieve, the country's history does not offer much hope. It is not clear that structural dysfunction inherited from Soviet times has been successfully addressed. And the astronomical level of corruption seems to be an impediment to achieving any real progress.

And so when McCain and his cohorts revved up the crowd on Maidan, what were they thinking they all would accomplish? What was this all about, really?

Look what the intrusive foreign misrepresentations have done to the poor Ukrainian people.

They were just honestly in search of a better life. What they got is a country that is now smaller, a civil war that has scarred the

country's soul, and an aid package that is
mistargeted and not up to the real job at
hand.

# Chapter 4

# Is the New Regime Legitimate?

*Was there a democratic transition or a coup staged by thugs?*

**AFTER** president Yanukovych fled Kyiv for his life, there were widespread news reports that he had been impeached.

But Radio Free Europe/Radio Liberty revealed that he was not.

In a story titled "Was Yanukovych's Ouster Constitutional?" the U.S. government sponsored international broadcaster documented that the efforts to impeach him fell short of the constitutionally required vote.

This really caught my interest because it reported facts that I saw nowhere in the mainstream media.

According to the RFE/RL story, "A majority of 328 lawmakers of the 450-seat parliament voted on February 22, 2014 to remove Yanukovych from power." It goes on to observe that the constitution calls for "a review of the case by Ukraine's Constitutional Court and a three-fourths majority vote by the Verkhovna Rada -- i.e., 338 lawmakers." That vote margin didn't materialize, and the required court review never took place.

Speaking on *The Daily Show with John Stewart*, Barnard College professor Kimberly Martin remarked, "They didn't quite follow the procedures constitutionally when they got rid of Yanukovych."

So there was no impeachment.

That didn't stop world media outlets from reporting on Yanukovych's impeachment, though.

Al Jazeera reported unequivocally, "Ukraine President Yanukovych impeached." The *Toronto Star* wrote, "Ukraine's future hangs in the balance as Yanukovych is impeached..." Even the *Kyiv Post* claimed, "Parliament votes 328-0 to impeach Yanukovych..."

Fox News wrapped it all up with this: "Yanukovych, who fled Ukraine's capital, Kiev, Saturday after being impeached by the country's parliament, defiantly insisted that he remains the legitimate leader of Ukraine."

But there really was no impeachment. It was all a phony story.

Did the impeachment myth originate with the new regime, or was it entirely a media concoction? I wonder.

## Yanukovych Was Not Impeached

It's a clear fact that the constitutional threshold for impeachment definitely was not met. Didn't any of the news organizations check their facts? Aren't they concerned about misleading their audiences?

In an attempt to learn the new regime's official position on this I called the Ukrainian mission to the United Nations. I talked to spokesperson Yegor Pyvovarov. He affirmed that Yanukovych was not impeached. Couldn't the news organizations have sought confirmation from Pyvovarov or his colleagues, too? What's wrong with these so-called news outlets?

But if Yanukovych was not impeached, what happened to him?

I asked Pyvovarov that question, too. He readily explained that the constitutional procedure for impeachment is quite onerous. Instead, he said, Yanukovych was removed because he "left his constitutional duties." That notion was backed up by Olexandr Motsyk, the Ukrainian ambassador to the United States. In a letter to the U.S. Congress, he said, "Yanukovych fled the capital and de facto removed himself from his constitutional authority."

Does that mean Yanukovych quit? The Fox News report has Yanukovych claiming he's still president. Many other outlets carried the same message. According to Yanukovych, he didn't remove himself from power.

So, did he or didn't he?

It turns out it doesn't really matter whether or not Yanukovych abandoned his post.

I found that the only way he can relinquish his office on his own would be if he "personally announces the statement of resignation at a meeting of the Verkhovna Rada of Ukraine," according to the constitution. Yanukovych never appeared before that body to resign. Yet the credentialed ambassador of Ukraine tried to tell the American Congress that Yanukovych left office through his own doing. It's hard to believe that the ambassador never read the constitution. But his message was a lot of bunkum. I wonder how many naive Congress members were sucked in by his misrepresentations. The multitude of media organizations sure were.

How are we to know what is really happening in Ukraine if prominent news outlets are clearly presenting falsehoods? Isn't it curious that a fabricated account of how Yanukovych was removed went mainstream? Who could possibly benefit from these news distortions?

## Unconstitutional Succession

Following the illegal removal from office of Yanukovych, parliament voted to install Oleksandr Turchynov as interim president.

That too was an illegal move.

The constitution provides that a vacancy in the office of president is to be filled by the prime minister. So even if the new regime's contention that Yanukovych's removal from office was legal, their next step, i.e., appointing Turchynov as interim president, was not.

There is no constitutional provision for any such thing as an interim president. If the constitution had been followed, Prime Minister Serhiy Arbuzov would have been called upon to execute the duties of the president.

## Constitution Removed Illegally, Too

The unconstitutional presidential switcheroo is not the only unconstitutional action of that new Ukrainian regime. Not only did it throw out Yanukovych, it also threw out the constitution. According to Ambassador Motsyk's letter to Congress, the Verkhovna Rada "restored" the 2004 constitution.

From what I can see, the extant constitution had no provision for "restoration" of a previous version. Indeed, the amendments that brought about that 2004 version of the constitution were subsequently declared unconstitutional by Ukraine's Constitutional Court.

So the new regime has unconstitutionally reverted to a version of the constitution that had already been declared unconstitutional. This all seems quite chaotic.

The constitution has a procedure for amendment, however. If the regime believed it necessary to change the constitution, couldn't it have followed the prescribed procedure?

Actually, it couldn't have.

You see, the constitution also says, "The Constitution of Ukraine shall not be amended in conditions of martial law or a state of emergency." Parliament had proclaimed the existence of "circumstances of extreme urgency." Without mincing words, there's little to refute that the country had been in a state of emergency. That meant no constitutional amendments at that time.

## A Mandate for Change Nonetheless

There may be little for the new regime to hang its hat on, constitutionally, that is. Does that make the leaders criminals who should be punished? Or is there a point to the regime change idea?

I've talked with a number of Ukrainians who believe that it was indeed time for Yanukovych to go. There are stories of pre-election promises that grossly were not lived up to. And rhetoric abounds about monumental corruption and personal enrichment by Yanukovych and his family and associates. And the country suffers under terrible economic conditions.

So there very well may be a mandate for change. And constitutional remedies may have been inadequate. It's said that Yanukovych's hold on the Verkhovna Rada stood in the way. Other countries facing a similar dilemma have indeed chosen a revolutionary path.

## Phony Characterizations

There's a nagging question about all this, though. If a revolution is all that justifiable, why are so many people avoiding the "r-word"?

Many media reports and comments by officials persist in characterizing what happened as a democratic transition.

*Item*: British deputy Prime Minister Nick

Clegg asserted that "the Ukrainian people rose up, as many did on the streets of Kiev, against their government seeking to claim greater democracy, greater freedom."

*Item*: James Rupert, an editor with the Atlantic Council spoke of "Ukrainian protesters struggling to pull their country toward greater democracy."

*Item*: Obama spokesperson Laura Lucas Magnuson lectured Russian officials for not supporting "the desires of the Ukrainian people for greater democracy and a closer relationship with Europe."

Yet what really happened was the deposing of a democratically-elected president, an unconstitutional seizure of power, and the cancellation of a democratically adopted constitution. What Ukrainians really got was a trumped up constitutional transition cloaked in falsehoods and trickery. In reality it was a transition by verbal sleight of hand.

"A group of persons controlling a government especially after a revolutionary seizure of power" is what *Webster's* calls a junta. That's what Ukraine's new government appears to be, a junta.

Instead of the clumsy trickery of the new regime, perhaps the leaders simply could have come clean and admitted that a revolution has taken place.

A lot of observers already had considered what happened in Ukraine to be a revolution. Shouldn't the regime have owned up to it and sought recognition of their revolutionary leadership by other countries and international organizations?

Whose interests are being served by presenting us with a distorted picture of what really happened? Is this an example of an intrusive agenda from abroad?

## Thugs in Their Midst

One theory I've heard for why the revolution was covered up has to do with who was involved. There is evidence that some recognized unsavory characters and organizations were within the revolutionary movement.

I'm not simply talking about deadbeats or guys with scruffy beards. I mean real bad guys. Fascists and neo-Nazis. I'll give you more information about them in a later chapter.

But, we don't hear much about those guys in most media reports. And the Obama administration is tight-lipped about this. Nonetheless there is credible evidence to back up the notion that recognized thugs were in the transitional Ukrainian government. It's too early to tell how many there are in the post-election crew.

## The Myth of Central Control

Gordon Hahn, an analyst for the Geostrategic Forecasting Corporation, suggests the government itself is even less unified than it appears. Writing in July, 2014 he reports, "There are at least four and potentially many more separate loci of power competing with Kiev for the claim of sovereignty to rule on the territory of post-Crimean Ukraine."

He explains: "Power now is being picked by various nationalistic and oligarchic warlords, who are establishing competing power centers. Few of these are tightly subordinate to the central government in Kiev now headed by President Petro Poroshenko and Prime Minister Arseniy Yatsenyuk."

## An Image Makeover Needed

By misrepresenting their revolutionary accession to leadership as a constitutional transition, the new regime started out on the wrong foot. Soft peddling the presence of fascists and neo-Nazis in their midst amplifies the problem. Most Ukrainians are not fascists. But, fascists have been permitted a role in the revolution. The distrust generated by this is only heightened by the puzzling complicity of the U.S. in the charade.

Many Ukrainians have shown great courage in ousting the former government, which they believed was propelling their country along a negative trajectory. Now it remains to be seen if the new leaders will have the courage to clean their own house and function with transparency and an absence of deception. Achieving real legitimacy will require that the new government be populated by patriots and competent leaders, not thugs with antisocial agendas.

# Chapter 5
# U.S. Position Fell Apart Quickly

*Did America make an unprincipled attempt to whitewash what just happened?*

**"THE** principles here are inviolable and they are starkly clear," Obama spokesperson Jay Carney told reporters about the crisis in Ukraine on March 10, 2014.

But the Obama administration clearly didn't stick to its guns. On one hand it renounced the then-upcoming referendum on Crimea's future, proclaiming that "it will not be viewed as legitimate because it is inconsistent with the Ukrainian constitution." Then days later, Obama met in the White House with Arseniy Yatsenyuk, the new Ukrainian prime minister who came to power by extra-constitutional means.

Why was the constitution overridingly important in one case, but not in the other?

Apparently for the Obama administration, the word "inviolable" is not inviolate. It's flexible enough for Obama to welcome a neo-Nazi collaborator to the White House.

## Just to Review the Background...

The rise to power of Yatsenyuk and interim president Olexandr Turchinov was unconstitutional because someone else was still the legal president. That was Victor Yanukovych, the wildly unpopular figure who was the principal target of the spectacular Maidan demonstrations.

The entire Maidan saga played out amid whispers that the U.S. and the EU were inciting discontent from behind the scenes.

U.S. support persisted as the crowd turned violent, hurling fire bombs and bricks at the police. The violence reached a crescendo when sniper fire broke out, killing and injuring many. At first demonstration leaders blamed the government for that. Then an Estonian government official raised suspicion that the snipers were hired by the protest leaders. After that the protest leaders switched their story, now blaming Russia. There still isn't a definitive answer.

One reliable source told me he learned from a high-ranking Ukrainian that the snipers were from Academi (formerly Blackwater, a private military and security services company). According to this account the sniper team came by boat and left on a Lufthansa flight to Stuttgart. The leader was a retired Navy Seal currently under the employ of Academi. The actual shooters were an assortment of Serbs, Balts, and Canadian Ukrainians. They used weapons that were locally sourced.

The whole sniper matter is still under investigation, and awaits a thorough explanation to set things straight.

**A Bungled Leadership Change**

Underneath all the Maidan tumult there may have been the germ of a good idea in calling for Yanukovych to go. And it's quite possible that a legal impeachment action could have succeeded eventually. And besides, the next presidential election was only a year away. Yanukovych could have been replaced democratically then.

But, instead, the revolutionaries chose to depose him extraconstitutionally. Despite widespread media reports to the contrary, as you now know, there was no impeachment. The leaders of the marathon street demonstrations just imposed themselves and took over. There was nothing constitutional about it. Yanukovych said his life was threatened and sought refuge outside the capital city, hoping that things in Kyiv would calm down. Meanwhile he still asserted that he was the legal president.

According to the protest leaders, though, the rule apparently is "out of town, out of office," because they claimed that Yanukovych's flight to safety was tantamount to resignation. But it wasn't. The constitution really does require a resigning president to appear personally before the parliament to tender his resignation. That never happened. Nonetheless, the new regime astonishingly represented their actions as being constitutional.

So now what we're left with is a new government that threw out the president and threw out the constitution -- and then got invited to the White House to meet with Obama. That invitation represents some dedication to inviolable principles, doesn't it.

## What about the Neo-Nazis?

The White House welcome had another troubling side to it. You see, the coalition government Yatsenyuk formed included fascist and neo-Nazi factions that had played a strong role in the street demonstrations. What I believe is especially controversial about this meeting is that the president has in effect invited a neo-Nazi collaborator into the White House.

Two factions, "Svoboda" and "The Right Sector," have come under particular international scrutiny. The Anti-Defamation League's Andrew Srulevitch has said that Svoboda has "a history of anti-Semitic statements to overcome, and a clear political program of ethnic nationalism that makes Jews nervous."

In 2012, the EU parliament passed a resolution calling Svoboda "xenophobic, racist, and anti-Semitic." Members of this faction were seen marching through the demonstrations wearing Hitler-era Nazi symbols. In the interim government Svoboda faction member Oleh Makhnitsky served as the Prosecutor General of Ukraine and member Ihor Tenyukh as the Minister of Defense.

Dr. Nicolai Petro, a University of Rhode Island professor while on research assignment in Ukraine, said "This Svoboda party has been rewarded instead of being marginalized. It was given four ministerial portfolios and several governorships as well as the Prosecutor General's office."

The Right Sector was a focus of a BBC documentary titled "Neo-Nazi Threat in New Ukraine." The report says it is perhaps the largest of the radical groups. Members have been seen on Maidan carrying baseball bats and guns. The narrator explains the bulk of Ukrainian demonstrators have been ordinary citizens, "people who simply refused to back down." However, "the most organized and perhaps the most effective are a small number of far right groups," the narrator asserts. Scenes are shown with participants marching through Maidan displaying their Hitler-era Nazi symbols.

BBC's reporter interviewed a representative about the Right Sector's political beliefs. The man responded saying "National Socialist themes are popular amongst some of us." That means, he said, "a clean nation ... not like under Hitler ... but in our own way a little bit like that." The Right Sector's leader, Dmytro Yarosh, became the Deputy Secretary of National Security in the interim government.

A well-informed expert observer told me, "It was clear at the start that from mid December, Maidan was hijacked by well organized 'lads in masks.' It was also clear that in order for the opposition to seize power blood had to be spilled."

On March 4, the *Guardian* published an expose titled, "Who exactly is governing Ukraine?" One of the new leaders, the report claims, destroyed documents in 2004 that allegedly suggested that Orange Revolution leader Julia Tymoshenko had links with organized crime. Another is widely believed to be behind "much of the protester-led violence -- including throwing Molotov cocktails and rocks at the police." And still another is described as an "an anti-abortion activist [who] once publicly suggested that women should 'lead the kind of lifestyle to avoid the risk of rape, including refraining from drinking alcohol and being in controversial company.'"

Also conspicuous among the leadership is the person who was in charge of the widely-reported protest camp at Maidan. The Estonian report still awaiting investigation alleges that the snipers that killed and injured so many had been hired not by the Yanukovych allies, but by the protest movement itself. Perhaps the shooting, characterized as a Yanukovych initiative, had actually been intended as a provocation for deposing Yanukovych.

Before the release of the Estonian report, the regime had been content with the widespread presumption that Yanukovych supporters were behind the sniper shootings. Afterward, however, they started to think otherwise. Regime officials floated the notion that Russia is to blame. The timing of the regime's reattribution seems to reveal a new-found need to shed blame.

Not all of the leaders reported in the *Guardian* story have questionable pasts. But the existence of radicals in among them may pose obstacles to international acceptance. And if it doesn't, it's worth asking why not.

## More Deception

Following Yatsenyuk's White House meeting, he gave a public presentation at the Atlantic Council, a Washington think tank. There he was asked about Russian president

Vladimir Putin's strategy vis-a-vis Ukraine. In his answer Yatsenyuk complained that, "probably president Putin doesn't know that this is the first government where a deputy prime minister represents the Jewish community. Then president Putin said some stuff about fascist protesters. No evidence at all. And we are the government who will fight with anyone who proclaims anything that resembles fascists or Nazis."

Given the presence of the Svoboda and The Right Sector factions in the Yatsenyuk government, it is hard for me to interpret Yatsenyuk's comments as anything but a bold lie.

The new Ukrainian regime has been dishonest about its unconstitutional rise to power. And it has swept under the rug the presence of fascist and neo-Nazi factions in its coalition.

I don't know what Obama talked about in his closed door meeting with Yatsenyuk. But doesn't he owe Americans an explanation of how he handled the Ukrainian extremist and dishonesty issues?

## Unreliable Journalism

And what about the reporters who listened to Carney's specious claim of inviolable principles, heard Obama's report on his meeting with Yatsenyuk, and observed Yatsenyuk's preposterous public presentation? Why haven't they called a spade a spade and signaled that something smells bad in all this?

This Ukrainian crisis started off being billed as a quest by the country to escape Russia's oppressive yoke and to seek a better future through association with Western Europe. But instead what we have is a triumph of extremist thugs and their collaborators, unsubstantiatable claims that they acquired power constitutionally, and a flat-out denial of the evidence that there were fascists and neo-Nazis in their midst.

The U.S. is apparently ignoring these strikingly large red flags. And there seems to be a huge head of steam behind the U.S. position. The media hasn't done its watchdog job. Even the ADL is capitulating. When I asked the organization to comment on Obama's taking a neo-Nazi collaborator into the White House, the organization waffled, claiming that Yatsenyuk had started "to unambiguously reject extremist Ukrainian ultra-nationalism." I've found no sign of that. And when ADL was asked substantiate its instant claim, the spokesperson declined to respond to the question.

What possibly could be the motive of these parties that have whitewashed what demonstrably happened in Ukraine?

# Chapter 6
# Sanctions

*What are they good for?*

**WHEN** in February through March 2014 the control of Crimea was moved from Ukraine to Russia it caused an enormous international stir.

An agitated Hillary Clinton exclaimed, "Now if this sounds familiar, it's what Hitler did back in the 30s."

A ready-to-fight John McCain urged: "Get some military assistance to Ukrainians, at least so they can defend themselves."

McCain's protege, junior Connecticut senator Chris Murphy, wailed that Putin has "done something incredibly stupid."

Amid all the histrionic rhetoric of the politicians, I went looking for the kind of hyperbolic news headlines that usually follow. But they were hard to find. The media played this issue relatively low key. The most jacked-up headlines I saw were:

--"Russia Stages a Coup in Crimea," the

*Daily Beast*
--"Ukraine Crisis: Crimea is Lost," the
*Independent*
--"Kremlin says Crimea is Now Officially
Part of Russia," *Washington Post*

Having seen the way wild and unsupported
accusations by politicians have been earlier
played up in the Ukraine saga, I found it
surprising to see a more reserved approach
here.

## What about Obama?

Obama was clearly in there with the other
politicians, though. Commenting on Crimea
he threatened: "It is not a done deal." Obama
explained, "Since the Russian intervention,
we have been mobilizing the international
community to condemn this violation of
international law and to support the people
and government and Ukraine."

In remarks given on March 6, Obama
proclaimed: "This morning, I signed an
executive order that authorizes sanctions on
individuals and entities responsible for
violating the sovereignty and territorial
integrity of Ukraine or for stealing the assets
of the Ukrainian people."

Russia responded in kind with its own
sanctions, targeting a number of American
political figures, John McCain among them.

The EU got into the act, too. On July 29,
USA Today reported, "...the European Union
imposed new 'sanctions' on Russia Tuesday
that they said will further cripple its
economy..." But according to international
legal expert Alexander Mercouris, "The EU
has no international legal authority to
impose sanctions without obtaining a
mandate from the UN Security Council."

All this sanctions activity set off a tit-for-tat
series of actions. In a sense, it is a non-
military war. One country, through sanctions
or other political or economic actions, seeks
to injure the other, and then the other
country retaliates. This cycle is on an
escalating trajectory. The stakes are growing
larger. The sanctions are not just confined to
the tit-for-tat war. There is a ripple effect.
They are causing economic damage around
the world, and are negatively impacting
people's lives.

Already, the result has been the greatest
setback in U.S.-Russia relations in years.
Things were looking up when George H.W.

Bush and Mikhail Gorbachev negotiated the end of the Cold War in December 1989. At that time, the leaders proclaimed "the beginning of a long road to a lasting, peaceful era" and the transformation of the bilateral relationship "to one of enduring cooperation."

Now, however, the relationship has devolved into one of mutual distrust and preoccupation with, frankly, a stupid regimen wherein each country is trying to injure the other through sanctions and other non-military means.

Dr. Edward Lozansky, president of the American University in Moscow asked U.S. Representative Dana Rohrabacher, "Does the policy of sanctions against Russia serve the best interests of the United States?"

Rohrabacher, a member of the House Foreign Relations Committee replied, "I don't think this is a situation in which the United States should have jumped in with full force behind one side or the other, especially in a way that could negatively impact both the economy and national security of our country. ...I think that imposing sanctions was a foolish thing to do."

It is not only foolish, it is also ineffectual.

I came across a study that calls into question whether sanctions have ever been an effective tool. It was conducted by the Institute for International Economics. The findings show the success rate has been in steep decline since 1970. By 1990 it was just 13 percent. And based on the cited rate of decline, I figure it's now down to 2.5 percent. That makes me wonder why everyone's so excited to use sanctions.

Obama once described his foreign policy mantra as "don't do stupid stuff." Methinks he should urgently apply that with regard to his own actions in the Ukrainian crisis.

## What about Putin?

I wonder: Did Putin or his advisors ever do a risk-benefit analysis regarding the reincorporation of Crimea into Russia?

Actually, I think that a legal argument can be made for the move. It happened at a time when there had been a collapse of constitutional authority in Ukraine.

In that vacuum, Russia took control of Crimea, and the revolutionary leaders in Kyiv attempted to take control of the rest of the country. It seems to me that each had or didn't have the same level of legitimacy. As it turns out, the Russian takeover was more peaceful than the other. As I write now, estimates are that thousands have died in the East from the civil war that ensued in opposition to the junta installed by the revolutionaries.

But the Russian justifications for the Crimean move do not seem to have been well thought out. They include claims that:

--Crimea was illegally taken from Russia in 1954 by Soviet leader Nikita Khrushchev, a man with close ties to Ukraine.
--Russians constitute the largest ethnic group in Crimea.
--People have always considered in their hearts that Crimea was part of Russia.

While these bear elements of truth, they sound to me more like wishy-washy rationalizations than legitimate justifications.

Given the constitutional vacuum that

existed, concerns for the integrity of Russia's naval base at Sevastopol, and sympathy for the Crimean ethnic Russian majority that was spooked by Kyiv's initial move against the Russian language, there was ample justification for some kind of action.

But quickly incorporating Crimea into Russia wasn't the only alternative. Couldn't Russia have taken temporary custody or stewardship of Crimea until stability in Ukraine could have been established by the revolutionaries, and until their final intentions on language and ethnic issues could have become clear? That would have addressed the instant issues. Such a response also would have held options open if things went poorly with the revolutionary government.

This course would not have invited the abject international scorn toward Putin or caused the economic damage to the country that has been done. Given the path that the Kremlin took, it seems to me that Putin must be saddled with some pretty poor political advisors and communication strategists.

## What about Ukraine?

Indeed, what about the Ukrainian people amidst all this back-and-forth sanctions nonsense between the United States and Russia.

In what way has any of it benefited the Ukrainians?

So far, the bottom line of the foreign attempts to help Ukraine is that Ukrainians have been given a fractured country, a bloody civil war, a humanitarian crisis with huge numbers of displaced persons and fleeing refugees, a bad economy made worse, and a revolutionary government that has not yet made an unambiguous break with the fascist and neo-Nazi elements that helped propel it into power.

# Chapter 7
# Paranoia and Aggression

*Indeed, who is paranoid and who is aggressive?*

**YOU** know the old joke, "I'm not paranoid, they really are out to get me!" Is that a line that Putin should legitimately use in his own defense?

There are quite a few observers who characterize his reactions in the Ukrainian crisis as paranoid. Just look at these headlines:

--"Vladimir Putin's Descent into Imperial Paranoia," *U.S. News & World Report*
--"Paranoia Leads Vladimir Putin to the Point of No Return," the *Telegraph*
--"Inside Vladimir Putin's Paranoid Vision," *BuzzFeed News*

What signals are given off by Putin that lead many to believe he is a victim of paranoia? He was even viewed as paranoid long before the start of the Ukrainian crisis. Reports I've seen say he was suspicious of a proposed American antimissile system that would have been installed at sites in Poland and the Czech Republic. He was alarmed by NATO's overtures to Georgia. And he believed that the EU's insistence that Ukraine choose between Europe and Russia was extremely problematic.

Of course there are more issues than these, but I think this sample will give you the gist of things. These reports characterize Putin's perception of threats. The other side of this is the American and Western European reaction that interprets Putin's positions as hostile.

## Is the U.S. Out to Get Putin?

In September, 2013, *Time* magazine wrote:

"So is Putin just a jerk? Maybe, although there are numerous reasons that might explain his antagonism: the lingering Cold War mentality of a former KGB agent; insecurity about Russia's post-Soviet global status; his sometimes comical machismo.

"There's likely another, potentially more important factor driving Putin's animus, however. He thinks we're out to get him. And in a sense, he's right."

Not only might he be right, but he is not

alone in his "paranoid" beliefs. From what I've seen personally, many Russians are suspicious of Americans. They think that the economic and political tragedies that beset them during the Yeltsin years were America's fault. They earnestly believe that the United States deliberately gave Russia bad advice on how to transition to a market economy and to a more democratic society. And they think it was all a scheme aimed at weakening Russia.

Was that mass paranoia? Or did *they* have a point?

I've never seen any concrete sign of a grand plan or conspiracy in the 90s that was intended to harm Russia.

Throughout that period, I followed very closely America's efforts to promote the emergence of press freedom and a viable media sector in Russia. Those programs never achieved that goal. But it was largely a result of American misperception of the problems and resultant mistargeting of the assistance programs. I don't think crippling Russia's media was the intended result. The help was simply wrongheaded.

For instance, there was one American NGO that had expertise in TV and radio production. It received massive U.S. government grants to help Russian media companies acquire better production equipment, learn how to use it, and also provided training in professional production techniques.

When it became unmistakable that none of that had really helped the media to become successful on their own, the NGO commissioned a study to find out why. An extensive business analysis was conducted of the media companies. What problem did it uncover that was impeding success? The media companies were spending too much on production! As a result, the NGO fired the guys that did the study and buried their report.

So it was true that the American assistance exacerbated rather than ameliorated the situation. But I don't think it was done maliciously.

That was just one example. In addition, I've talked with Americans who spent time offering Russian media managers business training for achieving greater success. In the end, the Americans would say of their students, "these guys just don't get it." And when I talked with the Russians, they would say of the Americans, "those guys just don't understand our situation."

## Ignorance plus Arrogance

I don't blame all this entirely on the American NGOs. The U.S. government agencies that controlled the funding bear greater blame. I know for a fact that they were offered proposals for interventions that were targeted at the heart of the media problems. But the funding agencies arrogantly stuck with the nonproductive programs. I go into greater detail on the nature of the media problems in my book *Medvedev's Media Affairs*.

The overall problem of ineffectual attempts in helping Russia was not limited to the media sector. It was pervasive in America's efforts to assist in other sectors, and in the selection of which Russian leaders to back. On a 2006 speaking tour of U.S. World Affairs Councils, Russian political and media analyst Alexei Pankin explained it this way:

"Unfortunately, in post-Soviet Russia, the

West threw its full weight behind people who were adventurers, thieves, market bolsheviks, robber capitalists. These people proclaimed themselves to be democrats. But, they were not. Their rule led to catastrophic consequences for the Russian economy, for living standards, and for people's self-esteem. It failed to create any stable institution.

"And all these failures, in the eyes of the vast majority of the Russian population, are now associated with Western support," Pankin concluded.

**NATO's Role**

With that as a backdrop, the U.S. also began pushing an eastern movement of NATO. It was viewed in Russia with great suspicion.

For one thing NATO was never created with friendship toward Russia in mind. The organization's first secretary general, General Hastings Ismay, said that NATO's goal was "to keep the Russians out, the Americans in, and the Germans down."

More than forty years later, on December 20, 1991, the *New York Times* reported,

"Russian President, Boris N. Yeltsin, wrote to NATO today saying Russia hoped to join the alliance some time in the future."

That never came to pass during Yeltsin's tenure. But in 2000, Yeltsin's successor, Vladimir Putin, publically dropped hints that he might like to see Russia actually become a member of NATO, too. But his overtures were rebuffed.

So it seems easy to understand how modern day Russian leadership might conclude that NATO's mission still holds to its original charter, "to keep Russians out."

That just might play a role in the paranoid-sounding rhetoric that we hear from Putin.

## Bamboozling Gorbachev

What's more, the U.S., whether deliberately or through bumbled diplomacy, actually tricked Soviet president Mikhail Gorbachev into thinking he had a deal that NATO would be contained.

Jack Matlock, a distinguished American diplomat, had been ambassador to the Soviet Union back then. He was actually in attendance at the crucial meetings that dealt with the end of the Cold War.

According to Matlock, the U.S. "had assured Russia during the debate on NATO enlargement that there was nothing to fear." He said the U.S. represented that NATO "was a purely defensive alliance, constitutionally incapable of undertaking offensive military action."

"We had earlier given Mikhail Gorbachev to understand," Matlock added, "that NATO's borders would not be moved further east if Germany were allowed to unite and stay in NATO."

But Russia ultimately saw a very different picture emerge. NATO did engage in offensive military action when in 1999 it attacked Serbia. And the organization certainly did move further east.

It took in Poland, Hungary, and the Czech Republic during the presidency of Bill Clinton. Under George W. Bush the floodgates opened. Bulgaria, Estonia, Latvia, Lithuania, Romania, Slovakia, and Slovenia came in. And to date under Barack Obama, Albania and Croatia have been admitted.

Meanwhile, Georgia, Montenegro, and Bosnia and Herzegovina are in the wings as aspiring future members. In late August 2014, Yatsenyuk announced a push for Ukraine to join.

## Inside the Machinations

This whole NATO issue concerned former senator Bill Bradley back in 2009. Writing in *Foreign Policy* magazine, he said, "The Russians insist that NATO expansion violated an explicit promise made by the first Bush administration; the Americans have not only denied it, but seem quite unaware of how much this dispute has haunted U.S. dealings with Russia."

Bradley relates how Gorbachev told him that U.S. Secretary of State James Baker looked him in the eye and said, "Look, if you remove your troops and allow unification of Germany in NATO, NATO will not expand one inch to the east." Bradley said he verified the accuracy of that report with Baker himself.

But according to Mary Elise Sarotte, a University of Southern California international relations professor, writing in the *New York Times*, Baker had gotten some pushback from the White House on his assurances to Gorbachev. As a result, President Bush wrote to German Chancellor Helmut Kohl with a clarification. It said, in effect, that there was no pledge regarding NATO's borders, Sarotte reports.

Apparently, no one thought to clear that up for Gorbachev, though. And thus was set into motion the expectation in Moscow that NATO would not advance toward it.

Bradley reflected, "Given President George H.W. Bush's earlier vow at the 1989 Malta summit that if Gorbachev allowed Eastern Europe to go its own way, the United States wouldn't take advantage, one can see how Gorbachev might have thought Baker was referring to any eastward expansion..."

But here's the key in all this: It shows evidence of a bamboozlement of Gorbachev. The fact that Bush felt a need to clarify the issue for Kohl demonstrated awareness of the ambiguity in the earlier communication. And the failure to offer that same clarification to Gorbachev suggests that the White House was okay with leaving Gorbachev with a false impression.

And therein lies the basis for Russia's belief that the U.S. acted with duplicity on the issue of NATO expansion. Matlock, writing in April 2014, diplomatically chalked all this up to "inconsiderate U.S. (and Western) actions met by Russian overreaction." His right-to-the-point view is that "all parties to today's current disputes bear some of the responsibility for the deterioration of relations."

That may be so. But if you look at today's reality through Russian eyes, what you see is NATO, an organization created to contain Russia, moving closer and closer to Russia's borders, in abrogation of what Russians had believed to be an agreement to not do that.

Matlock pulled no punches back in 1996. The House Committee on International Relations was considering U.S. policy toward NATO enlargement. Matlock warned the committee: "The closer NATO gets to the current Russian borders, the more the expansion is going to seem provocative to the Russian government. It seems to me there is no other way the Russians can read this. I don't necessarily excuse them for reading it that way, but think if the shoe were on the other foot and Russia were extending an alliance it dominated close to our borders, we would probably see it as a potential threat ourselves."

Putin paranoia? Or are they really out to get Russia and Putin, the country and the person? At best this is one colossally big misunderstanding that remains unsettled still today.

## Who's Paranoid?

Today, the American and Western European reaction to Putin's "paranoia" fails to consider the foregoing history when interpreting his reactions. Instead, these allies impute upon Putin their own interpretation that his motives and actions are threatening to the U.S. and its European partners.

In that light, it sort of puts the paranoia on the other foot, doesn't it. Who is it that seems paranoid now?

Looking at things from this perspective suggests that the U.S. and Europe have nurtured a deep-seated paranoia about Putin and Russia.

On August 27, 2014, the *New York Times* reported:

"Caught off guard by the crisis in Ukraine, NATO plans to create a "spearhead" rapid deployment force and a "more visible" presence in Eastern Europe to assuage concerns about Russian intentions, Anders Fogh Rasmussen, the alliance's secretary general, was quoted as saying on Wednesday."

Does this represent paranoia on the move? Or is it budding aggression?

## Aggression?

Russia may consider the proposed forward movement by NATO to be aggressive.

And NATO seems to be justifying its actions by what it claims is Russian aggression in Eastern Ukraine.

There is widespread acceptance of the notion that Russia is acting aggressively. Late August 2014 was awash in claims that Russia was conducting a military invasion of Ukraine. Typical headlines read:

--"Russia Has Already Invaded Ukraine: Strobe Talbott," *Huffington Post*, August 18
--"Russia Is Already Invading Ukraine," the *Atlantic*, August 25
--"Vladimir Putin's troops have invaded Ukraine," *Slate*, August 29

"This is a full-scale invasion," reported Mykhailo Lysenko, the deputy commander of the Ukrainian government's Donbas battalion.

## An American Observer

In the middle of this potentially world-changing invasion, New Jersey senator Robert Menendez, chair of the Senate Foreign Relations Committee, is found there on the scene giving a live interview to CNN direct from Kyiv. How ironic is that!

Interviewer Candy Crowley asks Menendez, "...just flat out, are Russian forces in Ukraine directly engaging Ukrainian forces?" Menendez replies, "Thousands of Russian troops are here with tanks, missiles, heavy artillery, and are directly engaged in what is clearly an invasion."

But Crowley didn't ask him if they were

engaging in an invasion. She asked specifically if the Russians were "directly engaging Ukrainian forces." Menendez flat out ducked the question, and Crowley let him get away with it. I wonder why Menendez wouldn't answer the question.

Crowley also didn't ask Menendez who told him that "thousands of Russian troops" plus tanks, missiles, etc., were engaged in an invasion. It doesn't appear he was an eye witness. Kyiv is over 400 miles away from where the "invasion" was taking place. Whose word did Menendez accept that it was really happening? Perhaps he had been privy to reconnaissance reports. Is that where he learned of Russia's aggression?

## Reconnaissance?

"Over the past two weeks we have noted a significant escalation in both the level and sophistication of Russia's military interference in Ukraine," reported Dutch Brigadier General Nico Tak, director of NATO's Comprehensive Crisis and Operations Management Centre.

Amid Russian denials of military interference, how did General Tak find out about Russia's military operating in Ukraine?

The *Daily Caller* had an answer. It ran the headline: "NATO Releases Satellite Photos Proving Russia Is Lying about Invading Ukraine."

"NATO Says Satellite Photos Support Claim That Russian Tanks Entered Ukraine," is how Mashable.com put it.

*Newsweek* claimed, "NATO Satellites Show Russian Troops, Armored Vehicles Inside Ukraine."

But Russia denied the authenticity of the photos. They said the images were faked.

I first saw one of the NATO photos on the Deutsche Welle website. It bore the name and logo of a commercial satellite imagery company named Digital Globe. I sent a link to that photo on the DW website to Digital Globe and asked them to confirm that the image was theirs. The photo bore their name. I just wanted confirmation that the photo wasn't faked. Digital Globe responded but refused to authenticate the image.

So I wrote to NATO about the image. An official there confirmed that NATO had distributed the images and said it was with the permission of Digital Globe. The NATO official shared with me a whole group of related photos, and assured me that the images they distributed are unchanged from what they received from Digital Globe.

So what we have here is this:

1. NATO distributed a group of satellite images, claiming: "New Satellite Imagery Exposes Russian Combat Troops Inside Ukraine." The photos bear the name and logo of commercial satellite imagery provider Digital Globe.

2. Russia calls the images fakes.

3. Digital Globe refuses to authenticate the images that bear their name.

None of this proves Russia's claim that the images are frauds. But neither does it inspire confidence that NATO's claims are on the level.

I confronted NATO with Digital Globe's refusal to claim the images as their own, and asked the NATO official if he could prompt Digital Globe to confirm the authenticity of the photos that bear the company's name. He responded saying, "Let me see what I can do." Now, months later, I've heard nothing further from either Digital Globe or NATO.

I'll leave it to you to decide what all this means.

But there's one other issue about the controversial images: One of the shots purports to show a Russian artillery battery on location in Ukraine.

By chance I ran across someone's blog comment that these artillery guns are in reality grain harvesters in a field. That prompted me to take a closer look at the photo, and to do some reality testing of the notion that NATO might have tried to pass off fuzzy images of grain harvesters as photos of artillery guns.

Because the analysis is somewhat tedious, I'm not presenting it here. Instead, you'll find it in Appendix III.

In the end, however, whatever you make of the sum total of the fuzzy NATO reconnaissance images, we seem to be left with a fuzzy picture of the alleged Russian military activity inside Ukraine.

Perhaps the one thing that is clear: the news reports and statements by the U.S. government and assorted Washington politicians that paint this situation as if it were clear, don't seem to have a clearly demonstrated basis in fact.

Indeed, they just might be false reports.

# Chapter 8
# False News Reports

*All the news that's fit to print?*

**THE** actual plight of Ukrainians is occluded from American and European audiences by the Western media reports about the crisis. The thrust of most stories about the Ukrainian crisis doesn't match the facts. The same can be said about statements made by U.S. government officials on the subject. As a result, we're unable to learn the facts from those sources.

I know it may be hard to believe that the mainstream story about the Ukrainian crisis is unreliable. But consider a few examples of verifiable factual disparities:

In Chapter 4 we examined the widespread reports that Yanukovych was impeached. For instance, on March 4, UPI reported "Yanukovych was impeached by Parliament a day after [an] agreement was signed, enabling the opposition to take control and appoint interim leadership."

This is a clear example of a news report that doesn't match the facts. To wit, my research shows irrefutably that he was not impeached. The Ukrainian mission to the United Nations attests to that. Yet news reports that said he was impeached have predominated.

Is this just an inconsequential technical difference? Isn't the main point that Yanukovych is gone, and it seems most Ukrainians are glad of that?

In terms of getting rid of the corrupt Yanukovych government, the point that he's gone is certainly important. But there is a bigger question here. It is: why is the news about Ukraine being so distorted? Why aren't truthful accounts being given? Why are things being misrepresented? Is there a nefarious scheme involved in that? Who is benefiting from the distortions?

**More Instances**

The impeachment example is not unique.

*Item*: A common thread in much of the coverage is the notion that the Maidan demonstrations grew from a passionate quest for democracy and a longing to escape oppression by Russia. In the *Telegraph* a

December 15, 2013 headline proclaimed, "Ukraine Would Be Enriched by Real Democracy."

But what facts could back up that claim? Back in 1997 then-American UN Ambassador Madeleine Albright told the Senate of a "deepening friendship with a democratic Ukraine." Was she fibbing? Did Ukraine not have a "real democracy"? She went on to point out that, "Ukraine was the first of the New Independent States to transfer power from one democratically-elected government to another." So not only was it democratic, it was an exemplary democracy in Albright's estimation.

Yanukovych came to the presidency by a democratic election that was generally regarded as fair and legitimate. What was not "real" about that? Simply because a president becomes very unpopular doesn't mean that democracy has been lost. Rather it means that voters made a poor democratic choice. The United States has had presidents who have become very unpopular. That never meant that democracy had evaporated. The same applies to Ukraine.

*Item*: On December 19, McCain told the

Atlantic Council that "a majority of Ukrainians -- not just in the West, but in the South and East as well -- see their future in Europe." But as I disclosed in Chapter 3, before the United States began influencing Ukrainians' freedom of choice, most Ukrainians by far did not support the EU initiative.

*Item*: The *Guardian* on February 23, 2014 claimed, "Demonstrators in Kiev are fighting for the things European Union countries take for granted -- freedom, democracy and peace."

I'm not sure what the freedom issue is here. But in terms of democracy and peace, the reality is that Maidan brought about the opposite:
--an unelected interim government,
--abandonment of a legitimate constitution,
--and civil war.

*Item*: The U.S. Defense Secretary inserted himself into the dialog, too. The *Washington Examiner* reported on May 23, "Hagel: Vladimir Putin Wants to Restore Soviet Union." That's quite a claim. It parrots a theme often used by McCain. I've looked hard for substantiation, but could find none.

Neither Hagel nor McCain have been able to back up their claims about a Putin agenda of conquest.

## Russian Expansionism

Many reports contain similar assertions that Russia wants to overrun Eastern Europe. Multiple times they have warned that Putin will not stop with Crimea. I don't know whether those allegations embody facts or not. But the individuals whose voices are behind those assertions don't really seem to know either. They present no verifiable facts. Why, they don't give us good reason even to suspect that their allegations have merit.

So, without any facts to back up their notions, the U.S. and NATO have made statements and taken actions that have inspired the fears of former Eastern Bloc countries.

For example, the *Washington Examiner* wrote: "Poland uneasy about Russian invasion after events in Ukraine." According to the *Daily Mail*, "Bulgaria and Lithuania fear they could be next on Russia's hit-list." Ominously, the *New Republic* asked, "Which Former Soviet State Could Be the Next

Ukraine?"

What are the likely consequences of Russia's alleged expansionism? According to financier George Soros, "Europe is facing a challenge from Russia to its very existence." That sounds worse than even the Nazi holocaust.

But the threat Soros describes is backed up only by his own suppositions and not facts.

The alarmist comments of Soros and the others offer no insights into the troubling tensions in the world. They just inspire fear and prompt ignorant reactions.

## A Real Threat?

Radoslaw Sikorski, speaker of the Polish parliament and former foreign minister, dropped a bombshell in October 2014 about Putin. He suggested the proof is in about Putin's alleged intentions of imperial conquest. Sikorski told *Politico* this all crystallized over the reversion of Crimea.

He explained, "This was the moment that finally convinced all doubters and turned all heads. This was Napoleon after Austerlitz.

This was Hitler after the fall of Paris. This was the moment that finally centralized everything into the hands of Vladimir Putin."

As background, Sikorski recounted a meeting that then-Polish prime minister Donald Tusk had in Moscow with Putin in 2008. Putin's proposition: "He wanted us to become participants in this partition of Ukraine," said Sikorski.

*Politico* concluded that "Russia has attempted to involve Poland in the invasion of Ukraine, just as if it were a post-modern re-run of the historic partitions of Poland." The *Financial Times* echoed the story: "Vladimir Putin had in 2008 suggested to former Polish prime minister Donald Tusk that the two countries could divide Ukraine's territory between them."

That sounds like a convincing indictment of Putin, doesn't it? It suggests that John McCain was right all along, that Putin is a ruthless dictator seeking conquest.

The only hitch is that Sikorski's story was a hoax perpetrated by Sikorski himself.

As his story began to fall apart, Sikorsky first

said his interview with *Politico* was "not authorized," and that some of his words have been "overinterpreted." The Associated Press reported that Sikorsky had become "vague about whether he made those exact remarks to *Politico*."

Sikorski then admitted that he had never personally heard of Putin offering to divide Ukraine, and refused to go into more detail or answer further questions.

At a subsequent press conference he said that indeed Tusk and Putin never even met in Moscow as alleged. The *Financial Times* now called this "a muddled denial and a full retraction" of what he said earlier.

So the whole tale initially told by Sikorski was just another example of a gratuitous attack on Putin that now has been proved to be entirely specious. I wonder if McCain knows about this.

## So What?

Clearly all the unsubstantiated reports of Putin's aggressive plans have caused reactions of fear. They've created a convincing illusion of a problem.

In turn, the U.S., one of the perpetrators of fear-inspiring false reports, stepped forth to offer solace and solutions. According to the *Daily Mail*, Vice President Joe Biden promised, "We're in this with you." And accordingly, the U.S. and NATO have sent in fighter jets, troops, and a variety of naval vessels to protect the region from the fabricated Russian threat. NATO started conducting military exercises in Western Ukraine. The *EUobserver* reported, "NATO reassures Poland, Baltic states on Russia threat."

Why does so much of the news about Ukraine advance concepts that are not backed up by facts? The real welfare of the Ukrainian people is getting lost in all the mixed agendas and information trickery.

So why are many of us believing the non-factual reports?

**An Explanation**

The answer, in part, is a phenomenon known as "confirmation bias." This is a psychological term for people's tendency to interpret information in ways that are partial to their existing beliefs, expectations, or hypotheses.

According to Tufts University research professor Raymond S. Nickerson:

"If one were to attempt to identify a single problematic aspect of human reasoning that deserves attention above all others, the 'confirmation bias' would have to be among the candidates for consideration. Many have written about this bias, and it appears to be sufficiently strong and pervasive that one is led to wonder whether the bias, by itself, might account for a significant fraction of the disputes, altercations, and misunderstandings that occur among individuals, groups, and nations."

What this means is when information confirms existing beliefs, it results in assigning credibility to that information, even if there is no apparent substantiation. Things that fly in the face of pre-existing expectations tend to be disbelieved.

Take this illustrative example: What would you think of a news report that Didier Burkhalter, president of the Swiss Confederation, had the tyrannical ambition of conquering Eastern Europe? Would you believe without substantiation that he was about to send tanks and troops eastward?

Of course you wouldn't. For one thing, you probably never heard of Didier Burkhalter. But even so, the notion that Switzerland would want to invade Eastern Europe would conflict with everything that you know about the country.

## Putin is Different

But what about Putin? You probably would find believable the story that Crimea was just his first stop in a march across Eastern Europe aimed at reestablishing the Soviet empire. That's consistent with all you've heard about the Russian leader. You've probably seen a lot of characterizations of Putin as a tyrant who will stop at nothing.

But what if those earlier stories about Putin were faulty? I'm talking about all the stories that go back years. What if they were as contaminated with inaccuracies as the faulty news reports on Ukraine? What if your expectations regarding Putin were based on false premises?

I'm sure this proposition must seem like

quite a stretch to you. Perhaps it sounds too wild to be true. It would take an awful lot of false premises to add up to the demonic reputation that Putin has acquired. How could deception on such a massive scale have gone undetected for so long?

The answer here is the same as the one for the false reports about Ukraine: confirmation bias.

Let's explore how this happened vis-a-vis Putin, and then extend that understanding to the Ukrainian crisis.

## Indicting Putin

Putin first appeared in the Kremlin as Boris Yeltsin's prime minister in 1999. Few Americans had ever heard of the man. His reputation was a blank slate.

I can remember following news reports about him back then. On one hand I heard Putin's own rhetoric that promised democratic improvements, restoration of pride in the country after years with the drunken Yeltsin in charge, and a fight to root out pervasive corruption. It sounded like a refreshing change from the crooked cronyism of the Yeltsin era. On the other hand there were cautionary reports warning that Putin was really a sneaky KGB alumnus who had the heart of a brutal dictator.

Those negative narratives persisted and intensified when Yeltsin resigned and Putin was appointed acting president.

When Russians would ask me what I thought of their new president, I didn't know what to say. Would he preside as the Putin of his own words? Or would he finally reveal himself as the tyrant some news reports alleged him to be? My doubts clearly had been inspired by the negative news reports.

Soon an avalanche of negative revelations appeared in the international press. They claimed Putin was actively rolling back the democratic achievements of Yeltsin and had put a clamp on Russia's free press.

There was one major flaw in that story that I instantly recognized. Russia hadn't had a free press for Putin to have clamped down on. In reality, there never was a truly free press under Yeltsin. At least not by normal Western standards, i.e., media that are free to tell the truth.

Yeltsin had instituted laws that made it virtually impossible for media companies to operate profitably and independently. That left them indentured to financiers who put money into the loss-making media enterprises in return for the opportunity to exert influence through the media on behalf of the financiers' own shady business or political endeavors. The media outlets were locked into the scheme.

I knew all this from personal experience. Since the start of the Russian Federation I have been involved as a business analyst and consultant in the Russian media field. I conducted a survey and analysis of Russia's media sector for the Association of Publishers and Editors of Russia. Later I did intensive work in 17 different Russian cities to help media companies there improve their operations. In addition, through my workshops and seminars, I also worked with hundreds of Russian media managers, literally from Kaliningrad to Kamchatka.

I've examined balance sheets and analyzed operations. And I can tell you that the vast majority of media outlets were not free in any Western sense of the word. They were financially conscripted by government officials and business tycoons. Those were the financiers. They called the shots on what the media would tell the public. The media were not free to tell the unvarnished truth.

Eventually I found that the stories of Putin nixing press freedom were actually malicious hoaxes perpetrated principally by two business tycoons that had extensive media holdings.

They had long used their control over the media to advance nefarious business deals of questionable legality. Mostly these schemes involved transferring valuable Russian state assets to their own hands for a small fraction of the real values.

When Putin tried to rein in that practice, the tycoons fought back with the allegation that he was oppressing press freedom. But on closer analysis, that allegation can be seen as false. The tycoons were simply using their media properties as weapons against Putin.

The whole press freedom story was specious. Nonetheless, Western media reports played it up. The U.S. Congress put forth a resolution condemning the crackdown. But there was no factual basis for any of those allegations. Putin may not have been a perfect president, but he wasn't guilty of the media crackdown as charged in the early 2000s.

A related fabricated story about the Russian media is that Putin was having journalists murdered who were in opposition to his tyranny. Perhaps you've heard that one. The allegation still persists in some media stories yet today.

But I checked the statistics of the Committee to Protect Journalists. The organization keeps a record of journalists killed in the line of duty. What I found is that year-for-year there were more journalists murdered during Yeltsin's tenure than Putin's. Almost twice as many. The CPJ statistics attest to that. Nonetheless, media reports continue to paint a picture that is opposite the reality. The truth is that there were fewer journalist deaths under Putin. And there is no evidence that Putin was at all involved in the journalist murders during his tenure. The "Putin is Killing Journalists" story is just another malicious fabrication.

## Where's the Confirmation Bias?

Now, I started this chapter on the theme of confirmation bias. But these early examples I just gave do not involve confirmation bias. They were simply smear campaigns. The stories were fabricated by political enemies of Putin's who wanted to discredit him.

The confirmation bias came in later. The initial fabricated stories laid the groundwork. They took the unknown Putin, whose reputation was a blank slate, and made him into a dangerous character. Or so he seemed.

So the false news stories sank in as the undisputed truth. Putin acquired a bad reputation. And it serves as a framework with which we interpret each new Putin story.

That framework is what psychologists call a schema. They say that once we have internalized a schema, our brain fights hard to protect and sustain it. That's because a schema is generally useful. It helps us to organize and interpret information. A downside occurs, however, when our efforts to protect a schema lead to rigidity. While we welcome new information that fits into the schema, when it doesn't fit we tend to either reject it out-of-hand or selectively interpret the new information to make it comply with the schema.

When it comes to Putin this means whenever we hear a new allegation, if it fits the schema we believe it even in the absence of corroborating details. Unfortunately, that leads us to accept fabrications as fact.

The Alexander Litvinenko story, a 2006 alleged murder by Putin, takes advantage of confirmation bias and schemas. But there's something more. It also invokes the use of archetypes, i.e., concepts that are universally imbedded in individual psyches. Litvinenko was characterized as a hero, a dissident. Putin was painted as a devil. Jungian psychologist Dr. Brian A. Shaw examined the story and concurred that it has been built through the use of common archetypes.

## Who's Doing the Fabricating?

Who was actually behind these fabricated, malicious stories about Putin?

I had no idea until 2007. That's when the

International Federation of Journalists commissioned me to investigate the media coverage in the poisoning death of Alexander Litvinenko.

The mysterious death of Litvinenko spawned headlines such as "Former KGB Spy Murdered on Orders of Putin." They cited a deathbed statement by Litvinenko that contained the accusation.

Ileana Ros-Lehtinen, a Florida congresswoman, and later chair of the House Foreign Relations Committee, introduced legislation accusing the Russian government of poisoning Litvinenko in London with a radioactive substance.

Ros-Lehtinen had called Litvinenko a dissident. Her resolution seemed to say that he was just one more dissenter that got rubbed out. Putin was widely pegged as the villain. The world viewed this Litvinenko story as factual.

But when investigating the media reports on behalf of the IFJ, I found that, contrary to popular opinion, the whole murder story was a fabrication. The news reports didn't match the facts.

Later, I wrote a book titled *The Phony Litvinenko Murder* based on my findings. In it I show that Litvinenko was not a spy, and he never worked as a secret KGB agent. What's more, the London coroner never deemed his death to be a homicide. And the deathbed statement? It turned out to be a fake. A former Soviet citizen later confessed that it was he who wrote the words, not Litvinenko. He also admitted there was no evidence to back up his accusation against Putin.

Yet to this day, it is popularly reported in the media that "former KGB spy Litvinenko was murdered on orders of Putin." But there is nothing in that statement that is factual. Nothing.

In July 2014, British Prime Minister David Cameron became a living demonstration of how insidious these kinds of fabricated news stories can be. At the height of the furor over the Malaysia Airline Flight 17 disaster he launched an attack at Putin based on the phony Litvinenko story. He had been taken in by the hoax about the dramatic deathbed statement that purportedly fingered Putin.

How could such a bold fabrication as the

Litvinenko fraud have been perpetrated upon the United States Congress, the Western media, the American public at large, and indeed upon the sitting British prime minister?

## The Culprit

The fabricator of the Litvinenko story turns out to have been a London-based former Russian, a political enemy of Putin's. He hired a top London PR firm to promote the phony story about Litvinenko. This initiative involved the same folks that decades earlier propelled Margaret Thatcher into the prime ministership.

According to widely-circulated news reports, the aim of Putin's political enemy was to replace the Russian government by force and violence. At first I found that hard to believe. So I contacted one of the journalists reporting the story. I asked who told him that tale. He responded that he himself had interviewed Putin's political enemy who made the allegation in the interview.

Later reports claimed that the enemy guy even wanted to install Prince Harry as a monarch in Russia.

Doesn't all that sound utterly preposterous?
But the story is a documented fact.

Yet this is the kind of nonsense Ros-
Lehtinen was taken in by. And she wasn't the
only one that was duped.

The "Russia Invades Georgia" and the Pussy
Riot stories are out of the same mold. They
were stories fabricated by Putin's enemies.

Here are some facts: An EU commission
investigated the Georgian war saga and
found that it was a provocation of Georgia's
not Russia's. I've seen that the foreign policy
advisor to John McCain's presidential
campaign had a direct connection to the
fabricated "Russia invades Georgia" story.
Isn't *that* interesting.

And the Pussy Riot case? Some of the same
people who concocted the Litvinenko
fabrication were in there pitching this
fabrication, too. I've seen documentary
evidence that rock stars were offered big
bucks to come out in support of Pussy Riot
by Margaret Thatcher's old PR agency. What
do you think of *that*?

Oh, and as to Ros-Lehtinen's notion that

Litvinenko was a principled dissident? The backstory is that he was actually in the employ of Putin's London-based political enemy. Litvinenko's occupation was to throw out journalistic bombshells. He accused Putin of blowing up Russian apartment buildings, being a pedophile, using energy as a weapon, and other dastardly deeds. All without corroborating evidence, of course. But many of us believed these fabrications. They fit the schema. Archetypes were invoked. There was confirmation bias!

## The Impact

If you have any lingering doubts about the possible impact on a population of persistent misinformation followed by confirmation bias, think of the Soviet Union. Russian journalist Dmitry Babich put it this way: "There was consistent propaganda working in the same direction from 1922 to 1941. A people's entire mindset changed. The prevailing psyche switched dramatically from Orthodox Christianity and liberalism over to Stalinism -- in less than 20 years."

The American and Western European media campaigns against Putin and Russia are now 15 years old and still running. And during that time the bounding glee toward Yeltsin's Russia as a welcome new partner has already been transformed into an adversarial feeling.

## Now Back to Ukraine

The horrible international reputation that was imputed upon Putin made work easy for those seeking to fool us regarding Ukraine. There was a strong confirmation bias involved. It seemed natural to most that Putin would have Hitlerian-type motives regarding Ukraine and Eastern Europe. In fact, some people actually likened Putin to Adolph Hitler.

Mincing no words, Lithuanian ambassador to the U.S., Zygimantas Pavilionis, told a World Affairs Council audience in October 2014 that "Putin is worse than Hitler."

A *Washington Post* editorial asked, "Is Vladimir Putin Truly a Modern-day Hitler?" It cited a comment by former Secretary of State Hillary Clinton comparing "the Russian president's excuse for invading Ukraine -- the 'defense' of ethnic Russians -- to Hitler's claim that he needed to protect ethnic Germans in Czechoslovakia."

*Forbes* magazine similarly asked, "Is Vladimir Putin another Adolph Hitler?" Under the subheading "Shades of Munich" it further inquires, "What's to Stop Putin?"

These stories play to Putin's well established negative reputation. It supports the false assertions that Ukraine had no democracy but was seeking it, and that it was trying to escape the oppressive yoke of Russia.

The big question, though, is why are people like Clinton and McCain making their cases against Putin with stories that are easily proved false? Perhaps they're counting on people's confirmation bias.

Their shenanigans are not benign, though. The false stories impede the ability of us all to make a realistic assessment of whether or not Putin is a threat.

**A Case in Point**

This is the case of men in beards: The Obama administration had been reporting that Putin sent military operatives into combat in Eastern Ukraine. As proof, a photo array was distributed in April 2014 by a number of U.S. officials. It included two shots of a bearded man in military garb. He is identified as a Russian special forces soldier. The caption claims one photo shows that man active in Georgia during the 2008 war with Russia. The other shows him in Ukraine in 2014. "These photos just show further examples of that connection," said Jen Psaki, a State Department spokesperson.

Simply put, the allegation was that a Russian military operative seen in Georgia in 2008 has been spotted taking part in the Ukrainian civil war. So the proof is in: Russian soldiers have been sent into Ukraine.

The only trouble is that the photos are of two different men in beards. The photos in the array were blurry with a low resolution. But even so, when I looked closely at the photos, there appeared to be two different men.

To get to the bottom of this, I clipped both images and entered them into Google's "search by image" function. That instantly located much higher resolution images of both bearded men. And clearly they were not the same man. The two people didn't even resemble each other. Even the beards were dissimilar. The State Department's proof was specious.

It took me less than five minutes to uncover the State Department's fraud. Didn't the people behind this caper realize that their effort to deceive could be detected so easily?

Perhaps they too were hoping for a duncical response from people who would unquestioningly believe the unbelievable if it were officially issued by the U.S. Department of State?

Well that's exactly what they got from the *New York Times*. On April 20, it splashed the headline "Ukraine Provides Evidence of Russian Military in Civil Unrest." The article included the photo array and said, "The State Department, which has also alleged Russian interference, says that the Ukrainian evidence is convincing."

Journalists Andrew Higgins, Michael R. Gordon, and Andrew E. Kramer in a bylined story on the same day repeat those allegations. A version of their story ran on page 1 of the paper's April 21 New York edition.

It must be that duncery attracts duncery,

judging from some of the online reader comments the latter *Times* story elicited. Here are just a few:

--"It is good to see hard evidence showing up for what we always knew was going on in eastern Ukraine."
--"I trust that no one is surprised by this, save for the usual pro-Putin/pro-Russia propagandists, that is."
--"It's time to demonstrate to the Kremlin -- and the Russian people -- that such a divergence from global norms has significant costs."

And all this in response to a story that was obviously suspect. This display of acceptance just affirms the "confirmation bias" phenomena that I described earlier in this chapter.

But not everyone fell for the ruse. There were skeptical comments as well. Here are a few examples:

--"Those photos look as convincing as the satellite shots of Iraq's WMD that the CIA presented just before the invasion."
--"Whether or not Russian operatives are in Ukraine, this evidence is a joke."

--"One of them could have been Santa if he changed his outfit and dyed his beard."

The skeptics made quite an impression with someone. That's because on April 24, a piece appeared from Margaret Sullivan, the paper's "Public Editor." It was titled, "Aftermath of Ukraine Photo Story Shows Need for More Caution." Well, there's an understatement!

Ms. Sullivan was quick to comment that the photos had been "endorsed by the Obama administration." But, she added, "More recently, some of those grainy photographs have been discredited."

So, after being caught prominently running a phony story, she tries to shed blame by pointing to the culpability of the Obama administration, and fingering the "grainy photographs."

But what about the *Times*' responsibility as a watchdog against government malfeasance? The dog must have died. And what about journalists Higgins, Gordon, and Kramer? They are experienced journalists. Why did they sully their reputations by putting their names to a garbage story out of Washington?

What about the *Times*' fact checkers?
Getting high resolution images to clarify the
"grainy photographs" required no more than
a series of mouse clicks.

And what about the *Times*' foreign editor,
Joseph Kahn? Actually, Sullivan gave him a
chance to speak for himself in her article.
She says he told her that "the *Times* has
made a major commitment to covering the
Russia-Ukraine story over the past several
months, using as many as 12 staff reporters,
many of them on the ground. He calls the
coverage 'voluminous, competitive, and
excellent.'" Isn't that incredible? The paper
makes a public arse of itself and Kahn calls
his team's work excellent?

Kahn hinted that the *Times*, in running the
phony story, "was not entirely dependent for
its conclusions on the photographs, but also
included other reporting that led to similar
conclusions." So he ran the rigged photos
without remarking upon their inauthenticity,
and expects us to believe whatever other
reporting they may have done? The story
was about the photos. That's what the
headline says. But he didn't mention that the
photos were fraudulent.

And what did Sullivan, the paper's internal watchdog, say about all this? She concluded that the "coverage of this crisis has had much to commend it" but that the story in question "was displayed too prominently and questioned too lightly."

Oy. They just don't seem to get it. None of them at the *Times*. What reason is there to believe future *Times*' reports?

And what about the State Department? Did they go down the drain on this one too?

They sure did. Ms. Psaki's retraction was even lamer than the *Times*'. Now she claims that the faked photos were only part of a "draft version" of a briefing packet. But at her April 25 press briefing, she clearly reported that the photos we now know to be fakes were provided publically by a number of U.S. officials. Speaking inconsistently does not seem to be problematic for Psaki. I don't know what kind of "draft version" she's talking about. But it's clear she wasn't telling the truth from the start. Why is that? Why did the State Department try to put one over on us?

## Who's Fighting Whom?

Accusations that Moscow is orchestrating the civil war in Eastern Ukraine are persistent, despite the disclosures about the fabricated bearded men story. Of course, the simple fact that Washington tried to hoodwink us on this doesn't prove that there are no Russians fighting in Eastern Ukraine. But it is strange and suspicious that instead of offering proof of the allegation, the State Department offered a fake story.

There's something else about who's fighting whom in Eastern Ukraine:

If Poroshenko believes he is fighting Russian troops there, and feels brave enough to engage them in bloody conflict, why has he not fought the Russian troops in Crimea?

It's not as if the Eastern Ukrainians attacked Kyiv. In fact it was Kyiv that initiated the fighting. The Eastern Ukrainians seem just to be defending what they consider is their own territory, whether justifiably so or not.

The fact that Kyiv launched the war in the East, and not on Crimea leaves open the puzzling question of why Poroshenko is

willing to fight Russians in one place but not
in the other.

Here's one hypothesis: He doesn't really
believe that he's fighting the Russian state in
Eastern Ukraine. But without his contention
that he's fighting Russians, it means he's
fighting and killing his own people, citizens
of Ukraine.

The notion of a leader "killing his own
people" has a long history of international
condemnation. I did a Google search on the
term "killing his own people." It turned up
names such as Bashar Al-Assad, Muammar
Gaddafi, Robert Mugabe, Saddam Hussein.
Is Poroshenko trying to avoid being
associated with that notorious group? Is he
trying to dodge that by inventing or
exaggerating Russians in the East?

The fact that he's not fought Russians in
Crimea suggests a tacit admission by
Poroshenko that under it all he knows he's
basically fighting his own people in the East.
This Russian stuff is likely just a subterfuge.

**The Humanitarian Crisis**

By July, 2014, stories were emerging about

the unfolding humanitarian crisis in Eastern Ukraine. UNHCR, the United Nations relief agency was reporting that enormous numbers of refugees were fleeing from Ukraine into Russia. However, at a July 1 Department of State press conference, when asked about the tragic cross-border exodus, deputy spokesperson Marie Harf trivialized the tragedy with the quip, "That could be to go visit their grandmother and come back."

Harf also quibbled with Russian sourced refugee reports cited by UNHCR, adding that State would "attempt to get alternative sources of information" to UNHCR. For their part, though, the UN agency maintained that it already had the story straight.

Reporting the truth on the cross-border refugee emergency, however, did not come quickly to UNHCR. It started off, like the State Department, denying the extent of the tragedy. In a May 20 statement it reported that "The number of Ukrainian asylum seekers in other countries has remained low."

That conflicted with first-hand accounts I had seen. So on June 6, I wrote to UNHCR spokesperson Adrian Edwards:

"In your 20 May briefing notes you report, 'The number of Ukrainian asylum-seekers in other countries has remained low.'

"Yet Konstantin Romodanovsky, head of the Russian Federal Migration Service has reported, 'About 4,000 Ukrainian nationals have asked the Russian Federal Migration Service for a refugee status or have applied for temporary asylum in Russia.'

"Do you have affirmative information that Romodanovsky's claim is inaccurate? If so, what is your source of information?"

Edwards didn't respond.

By June 9, further information came to my attention, and I wrote to Edwards again:

"Further to my earlier email, I just saw that the Macedonian News Agency reported last week:

"'On Wednesday the governor of South Russia's Rostov region stated that he was considering declaring an emergency situation because of the influx of Ukrainian refugees fleeing the combat zones.'

"This and the Romodanovsky comment I cited for you last week seems to stand in contrast to your report that 'The number of Ukrainian asylum-seekers in other countries has remained low.'

"What is the source of information for your statement?"

Edwards didn't respond again.

But by June 27, UNHCR had finally changed its story. Now it was reporting that increases are "being seen in the numbers of Ukrainians in Russia and other countries," and that "since the start of the year around 110,000 Ukrainians have arrived in Russia."

That wasn't the end of the story. On July 9, UNHCR finally let loose with the blockbuster report: half a million refugees were already in Russia after fleeing combat in Ukraine. And the number of refugees has greatly increased since then.

I asked UNHCR about the State Department "grandmother" story that discredited reports of refugees in Russia. A UNHCR spokesperson told me, "Our staff members travelled to the border areas. We have seen everything with our own eyes, and we have no reason not to trust the information provided by the Russian Migration Service."

So this is another example of the Obama administration misrepresenting the truth about Ukraine. I don't know if the State Department initially strong-armed UNHCR to keep the relief agency from telling the whole story. But for State to have characterized an epic flow of desperate refugees as people merely travelling to visit their grandmothers in Russia is not only deliberately misleading, but is an incredible display of callousness toward the frightened refugees.

But the nagging question remains. Why are they doing this? Why did the Obama administration again try to make its points with falsified information? If it has a case to make in favour of the new Ukrainian leadership and against Putin, why can't it be done in a fact-based way? Why are they resorting to falsification?

**Integrity**

Integrity is not something that is exhibited on a case-by-case basis. Either you've got it or you haven't.

We've seen time and time again that the Obama administration and indeed Washington politicians in general have been misleading us all regarding what is happening in Ukraine. The White House and the State Department have repeatedly put out patently false stories. So have House members and Senators. Media outlets like the *New York Times* have witlessly and unquestioningly reported the deceptive claims of the administration and American politicians.

That gives us little to go on when we try to interpret new incidents that arise.

For instance, the Obama administration has been actively telling us that Russia was directly behind the destruction of Malaysia Airlines Flight 17. It is also claiming that government-held positions in Eastern Ukraine are being shelled by weaponry within Russia proper.

No supportive evidence has been presented publically. Only indistinct references to classified information are offered. That's even less than we were given when the Bush

II administration was preparing us for launching a war against Iraq.

There just isn't any sensible reason to trust what the Obama administration and other Washington politicians have to say about Ukraine. They've demonstrated a lack of integrity.

So what's the truth about Flight 17 and the shelling from Russian territory? We just don't know. The Obama administration may be right that Russia is involved. But it has established a track record of lying about Ukraine. So we have no reliable information about what's going on.

That's been the case with the whole Ukrainian crisis. All we have are false news reports. But hopefully my analysis of those reports now will have shed light on what really is going on.

# Chapter 9
# Putin's Buffoonery

*Isn't it time for it to end?*

**IT's** one thing to recognize that much of Putin's international image has been constructed from fabrications advanced by his political enemies, foreign and domestic. But it's another thing to try understanding why he's taken no effective actions to straighten out the mess. His lack of effective response seems to defy reason.

Putin's inattention to the reputation of Russia and its leadership has led to a lot of misunderstanding and now even to human suffering. For instance, it is hard to envision how the U.S. and European victimization of Ukraine could have gotten off the ground were it not for the popular belief in Putin's dangerous nature.

Putin is certainly not to blame that political enemies have launched media attacks against him. But he is clearly to blame for not taking strategic steps to counteract the damage. In that regard, Putin has done more than any other person to engender Putin hatred. Not by his actions. Mostly by his inaction. His absence of any effective response to the persistent denigration of Russia and its leaders has done more to solidify the near-universal negative images that prevail than the work of any other individual.

## Enemies in Control

The problem is that for too long Putin has allowed his enemies to define him. They've been in control of his image. What's worse, many of his actions have strongly reinforced that negative image. I'm talking about the indiscriminate crackdown on NGOs in Russia; the mishandling of the Pussy Riot caper; and the signing of an adoption ban in retaliation for the American Magnitsky Act. Putin is being held prisoner within the villainous image his enemies have created.

It was one thing when he was just a victim of media attacks advanced by others. But it's a different story now that he's foolishly playing into the hands of his enemies.

By not acting decisively and effectively to the onslaught of negative attacks in the media, Putin has neglected his responsibility to protect the image of the country. All the negative media coverage isn't doing much good for Russia's position in the world and relations with the United States. It's resulted in Russia becoming an outcast state in much of the world and Putin being viewed as a villainous leader.

Putin seems oblivious to his own pernicious role in all of this. And apparently no one around him is willing to confront him with his own failing. So, he is left like a guy with bad breath surrounded by friends unwilling to tell him. When it comes to media relations, Putin has bad breath. Someone should tell him.

## Campaign after Campaign

Here are some examples of specious themes used in the successful media attacks against Putin:

--Using energy as a weapon
--Cracking down on press freedom
--Retreating from the democracy of the 90s
--Exhibiting pedophilic behavior
--Crushing dissenters
--Blowing up apartment buildings
--Killing journalists
--Murdering Litvinenko

--Invading Georgia

The attack in connection with the Sochi Olympics was especially egregious. America unleashed its heavy artillery when it announced an official Travel Alert to Americans. It said U.S. citizens "should remain attentive regarding their personal security at all times." The Alert justified itself with a litany of potential problems that under scrutiny turned out to be largely non-issues. This had all the appearances of a scare tactic. Obama announced that he wasn't going.

All that came in the wake of two highly-publicized terrorist events. The first was a series of two suicide bombings in Volgograd, Russia in late December 2013. The second was the discovery of six dead bodies in cars on the outskirts of Pyatigorsk, Russia in early January 2014.

Regarding the former, a CBS News report read, "Suicide bomber attacks near Sochi." CNN's version said, "Russia bombings raise questions about Sochi Olympics security."

On the Pyatigorsk incident, ABC News proclaimed, "Mystery bodies, explosives discovered near Winter Olympics site." The *Atlanta Journal Constitution* reported, "Russia launches probe after six found dead near Sochi."

## Fair Reporting?

These were certainly tragic events. But the media should have paid a bit more attention to their geography.

For instance, would a suicide bombing in the Italian Alps be a realistic worry for people at a large public gathering in Berlin, Germany? Or likewise an incident 100 miles north of Montreal to people in New York City? Those are examples of distances similar to the expanse between Volgograd and Sochi. That's what CBS news called "close."

In the other example, Pyatigorsk to Sochi? That's like Brooklyn, New York to Brattleboro, Vermont, or Munich, Germany to Alsace, France. ABC News and the *Atlanta Journal Constitution* both considered that proximity to be "near."

It's hard to imagine that journalists and editors at these media outlets are simply that out to lunch. I find it difficult to chalk-up these exaggerations to ignorance. I'd call them potshots.

**The Big Gun**

Then there's the State Department's cannon blast, the Travel Alert. Certainly, travelers should always be "attentive regarding their personal security" wherever they travel. It just makes sense. But why did the State Department make that the subject of an ominous sounding Travel Alert?

For comparison, I checked to see if similar alerts were active for other places in the world. I found at the time of the Sochi Olympics there were two. One was for Egypt over the "continuing political and social unrest," and the other for Madagascar, related to its election season. The stated reason was because, "gatherings intended to be peaceful can turn violent with little or no warning."

But the general instability that existed in those two troubled countries is a far cry from the security-controlled environment that was prepared for the Sochi Olympics complex.

Indeed, wouldn't security and control be

bywords of any Olympic venue past and future?

The United States had the experience of hosting the Salt Lake City Olympics in 2002. That was just five months after the 9/11 attacks on New York and Washington. Who in the United States believed at that time that the al-Qaeda threat had been eliminated?

I searched for press coverage from the months preceding the opening of those Games. I looked for reportage that suggested Olympic danger. There wasn't much. NPR reported on February 7, 2002, "When the Winter Olympics gets under way in Salt Lake City Friday, officials promise the heaviest security ever for a sporting event." (Keep in mind that the 2001 terrorist events killed about 3000 people.)

But on December 30, 2013, NPR carried this report: "Two suicide bombings in as many days have killed 31 people and raised concerns that Islamic militants have begun a terrorist campaign in Russia that could stretch into the Sochi Olympics in February."

Notice how the 2002 report has a reassuring

tone, whereas the 2013 report seems alarmist. The tonal difference in coverage seems to belie the relative death totals. What was NPR up to?

There's no doubt that the Sochi Olympics presented a unique security challenge. And disasters at previous Olympics show there is a concrete risk of tragedy. But the media have failed to take into account that Putin's political enemies have been taunting him with suggestions of violence during his showpiece Olympics, and urging boycotts. That failure in judgment led them to run fabricated stories warning of massive persecution of gays, a likelihood of terrorist attacks, and promising the humiliation of having to use toilets that were built two to a stall.

None of that came to pass.

Little journalistic scrutiny had been used to differentiate between credible physical threats and the promotion of fabricated stories intended for using the media as a weapon. Overall, the news coverage I saw suggested a goal of fomenting alarm, instead of simply reporting the facts.

## Opportunism Abounds

No one should be surprised that media-based attacks against Russia and its leader would grow stronger during the Olympic season. Past media attacks, organized by Putin's political enemies, have been opportunistic and also founded upon fabricated allegations. Crusading journalist Anna Politkovskaya was killed on Putin's birthday. The initial media blitz over reputed former spy Alexander Litvinenko's poisoning in London occurred while Putin was attending the Asia Pacific Economic Cooperation Summit in Hanoi. The focus of the attendant news stories involved accusations of Putin's culpability.

And speaking of timing: The grand closing ceremonies at Sochi on February 23, 2014 were overshadowed by the tragic February 20 mass killing in Kyiv by mysterious snipers allegedly sent by the "pro-Russian" Yanukovych government. Putin's enemies struck again.

## It Could Have Been Different

Putin controls a vast media operation geared to external communications. They include print, broadcast, and online. And he has world-class public relations advisors. Much of the external communications offerings are well done and provide an alternative point of view for international audiences. None of that, however, adds up to what's required to effectively remediate his international reputation. To believe that it does, reveals a lack of understanding of the problem.

Specialized resources have been offered to Putin for targeting the reputational issues with advanced techniques. As early as October 2012, efforts were made to draw the Kremlin's attention to the impending Olympics media problem. "Russia without Spin," a Russian-American private sector initiative that I strongly support, was offering to help with its specialized expertise.

But it was hard to find friends in the Kremlin for this project. Those within the administration, and some leaders of its communications arms, ultimately seemed not to care about solving the problem. They appeared more focused on simply assuring their share of the state budget, even though the problem of Putin's terrible international reputation would go unaddressed in any serious and effective way.

In response, Russia without Spin undertook a demonstration to show the efficacy its proprietary skills in counteracting news reports that are founded upon fabricated information. The Litvinenko case was ideal for that purpose. It involved a high-profile British search for alleged Russian culpability, albeit with an absence of any substantiating facts. In the end, the Russia without Spin initiative was successful in its advocacy for ending the specious search. The quest for Russian culpability was cancelled and the Litvinenko topic was taken out of the news, at least for the time being.

At that time, we warned that the Litvinenko story might flare up again in the future without continued attention. But again, the Kremlin was not responsive. We pointed out that Putin and Russia would "continue to be victims of the typical malicious media attacks they have sustained since the beginning of Putin's leadership in Moscow." We said that it's hard to see how that will help anyone other than Putin's political enemies.

**And Now Ukraine**

The U.S. and the EU could not have

launched their dangerous game in Ukraine without an ability to convince the world community that Putin is a treacherous tyrant and an immediate threat to Russia's neighbors.

What happened in Ukraine epitomizes the foolishness of Putin's inattention to the international reputation of Russia and its leadership.

All the deaths in Ukraine -- from the Maidan riots to the civil war -- and all the economic damage to Russia itself as well as to the greater world community are fruits of this inattention.

While Putin bears ultimate responsibility, he is not singularly to blame. Those in his inner circle who have responsibilities connected to reputational problems have clearly disserved him.

Isn't it about time that Putin reassess what he is doing on the reputational front and follow a more responsible path, one paved with more efficacious strategies and techniques?

Isn't it time to stop the buffoonery?

# Chapter 10
# Making Sense of It All

*Who's to blame, and why did they do it?*

**IN** previous chapters I've documented that much of the news we've seen about the Ukrainian crisis has been distorted by fabrications.

You've seen that "confirmation bias" explains why many of us believed the fabricated stories of Putin's evil intentions regarding Ukraine and the rest of Eastern Europe. It also explains why many of us believed the fabricated bearded men story instead of our own eyes, for instance.

And you've seen how the Obama administration has demonstrated a lack of integrity in releasing information about Ukraine. It is deceiving us. So are many other Washington politicians.

But that doesn't explain why they're doing that.

It's worth asking: Who is in a position to benefit from misleading the world about the Ukrainian crisis?

Who has a motive? Indeed, showing who has motive can be helpful in confirming the identity of the perpetrator or perpetrators.

The purpose of this chapter is to find those answers by analyzing the evidence. That process will entail delving into some statistics, logic, and history, and analyzing texts. This may seem laborious at times. But it will be worth wading through. That's because at the end you'll find a new understanding about what this crisis has been all about.

## So Who Did It?

Various media organizations have played a role in exposing us to the kind of reports I've shown to be fabrications. Did those organizations conspire to pull the wool over our eyes? Many casual observers jump to that conclusion. They reason that because we got the false accounts from the media, it must be that the media are the perpetrators.

That explanation is inadequate on several counts.

First of all it would require a massive conspiracy and would have involved many conspirators. They would include media executives, publishers, producers, editors, journalists, and sources. The likelihood that such a vast conspiracy could be kept secret would seem remote. It's hard to keep a lid on a vast conspiracy. Trying to do that was the downfall of Richard Nixon in the legendary Watergate affair. In the end, that attempted conspiracy was revealed to all.

Second, we're talking now about media outlets that are commercial competitors. If one outlet were giving its audience false information, competitive incentives would encourage other outlets to expose it. That's a strong motive that augurs against collusion.

And finally, if there really were a conspiracy among world media outlets, it would have to have a coordinating mechanism. There would have to be some center of control to orchestrate the perpetration of such a massive fraud on the public. I've seen no evidence of any such command structure. Have you?

**Blaming the Messenger?**

Blaming the media amounts to blaming the messenger.

I realize that media outlets are not just simple messengers. They're not supposed to repeat unquestioningly whatever they hear. The media have an obligation to their audiences to fact-check the news they are delivering.

In that respect the media certainly do deserve blame and condemnation for what has been clearly a lack of responsibility or outright incompetence. I've shown that the *New York Times* is a prime example. But the idea that media originated the stories doesn't fit the facts and circumstances. Media organizations didn't start the ball rolling.

Then who did?

## The White House?

In earlier chapters you've seen that information propounded by the Obama administration doesn't jibe with the facts. The bearded men story shows that clearly. But could the White House have been behind much more of the false information? Let's examine the possible role of the Obama administration in the fabrications about the Ukrainian crisis:

At first the United States pointed to the illegitimacy of Ukraine's new regime based on constitutional grounds. Next it rejected the legitimacy of a referendum about Crimea's future, calling it unconstitutional. And then it embraced the unconstitutional new Kyiv regime, considered it legitimate, and promised it great support. The original and valid analysis that the regime change was unconstitutional just fell by the wayside.

Judging from its actions and comments, the administration's position has been to gloss over:
--the use of violence and lawlessness on Maidan
--the unconstitutional assumption of power by the new regime
--the throwing out of the legitimate constitution
--the inclusion of fascist and neo-Nazi factions in the interim government

## Talking Points are Double Talk

The U.S. position embraces the pretense that the Ukrainian crisis grew from the Ukrainian people's passionate quest for Western democracy over Russian oppression, and that the new leaders have formed a

constitutionally legitimate government.
You've seen here that those contentions are
not true.

The White House actually put out a talking
point defending its revised position that the
new regime was legitimate:

"Mr. Putin says: Ukraine's government is
illegitimate. Yanukovych is still the
legitimate leader of Ukraine.

"The Facts: On March 4, President Putin
himself acknowledged the reality that
Yanukovych 'has no political future.' After
Yanukovych fled Ukraine, even his own
Party of Regions turned against him, voting
to confirm his withdrawal from office and to
support the new government. Ukraine's new
government was approved by the
democratically elected Ukrainian
Parliament, with 371 votes -- more than an
82 percent majority. The interim
government of Ukraine is a government of
the people, which will shepherd the country
toward democratic elections on May 25th --
elections that will allow all Ukrainians to
have a voice in the future of their country."

If you didn't know any better, you'd think

that "The Facts" convincingly refuted claims that the interim government was illegitimate. But every sentence in that talking point either commits a logical fallacy or misrepresents the facts, or both.

Can you identify the fallacies and misrepresentations?

**Talking Point Analysis**

Here is my sentence-by-sentence analysis:

*White House "Fact"*: "On March 4, President Putin himself acknowledged the reality that Yanukovych 'has no political future.'"

*Analysis*: This statement attempts to discredit Putin's contention that at the time Yanukovych was still the legitimate president. To state the White House argument syllogistically, it would be:

--A president who has no political future is not a legitimate president (premise)
--Whatever Putin says about a president's future is true (premise)
--Putin says Yanukovych has no political future (premise)
--Therefore Yanukovych is not a legitimate

president (conclusion)

This is an internally consistent argument. But the first two premises are clearly false. I would wager that at this very moment there are around the world multiple heads of state who have no political future in the minds of some. But that in itself is not determinate of whether or not a president is legitimate. And who really believes that whatever Putin says about any president's future is necessarily accurate?

The "real fact" is that whatever Putin thought about Yanukovych's future has no bearing on whether or not Yanukovych's presidency was legitimate. The White House statement is an argument based on false premises.

(Technically speaking Putin was right. According to the constitution Yanukovych was still the legitimate president. That does not mean that in a practical sense this reality was a good thing. There is reason to consider that the revolution could lead to a better outcome for the Ukrainian people than following the constitution. But instead of simply stating that, the White House uses tricks of logic as a form of subterfuge.)

*White House "Fact"*: "After Yanukovych fled Ukraine, even his own Party of Regions turned against him, voting to confirm his withdrawal from office and to support the new government."

*Analysis*: This statement commits the "appeal to authority" logical fallacy. It argues in effect that (1) the Party of Regions has the authority to confirm a president's removal from office, (2) its support of a new government lends legitimacy, and (3) if it says something about those matters, it is probably true. But the "true fact" here is that none of that is true.

The Party of Regions has no official role at all in legitimizing a claim that Yanukovych was removed from office. You saw in Chapter 4 that his removal from office was unconstitutional. And a vote by the Party of Regions to support the interim government gave that regime no constitutional legitimacy at all.

It would be good if the Party's vote were reflective of a consensus emerging to support the revolutionary government, and if that government would truly serve the Ukrainian people. But instead of coming out and saying that, the White House continues to mislead and misrepresent that which was unconstitutional as being constitutional. And it twists logic to make its points. That leads me not only to wonder what the administration's motives are, but also to suspect that something underhanded is behind all this.

*White House "Fact"*: "Ukraine's new government was approved by the democratically elected Ukrainian Parliament, with 371 votes -- more than an 82 percent majority."

*Analysis*: By this time, there was no legitimate governance in Kyiv. The elected president and democratically enacted constitution were thrown out by revolutionaries. That left a constitutional power vacuum. And in that vacuum, the revolutionaries took over in Kyiv, and Russia took control of Crimea. Yet the White House persists in misrepresenting what happened in Kyiv as a democratic process. If there was no legitimate government at the time, an 82 percent majority has no meaning. The May 25 presidential vote lent credibility to the new revolutionary government. It was a vote in effect to legitimatize the revolution. But

Washington's persistence in pretending that there was initially a democratic transition imposes a level of nonsense. It's hard to understand why the administration is doing that. I think it would be better if Washington would simply recognize the revolutionary government as the will of the people. Or at least most of the people.

*White House "Fact"*: "The interim government of Ukraine is a government of the people, which will shepherd the country toward democratic elections on May 25th -- elections that will allow all Ukrainians to have a voice in the future of their country."

*Analysis*: There they go again. The term "government of the people" is popularly thought to define a democracy. You've seen that the interim regime in no way achieved control through democratic process. But we're now post-May 25 and a new president was elected by a vote that so far seems to have been largely uncontested. Let's hope that president Poroshenko will have the sense and the strength to weed out the fascists and neo-Nazis who were in the interim government, and assemble a team that can work for the good of all Ukrainians.

## What's the U.S. Game Here?

What in the world is the U.S. trying to accomplish with all of its manipulation of the truth? You can see the level of deception used in the talking point that I just dissected. That wasn't the only phony talking point. There are others. And the collected set of talking points isn't the only initiative of the Obama administration to create a narrative about what's happening in Ukraine that severely distorts the truth. You've seen other examples in earlier chapters. It's been distort, distort, and distort, all the time.

Earlier I raised the question of who's behind the fabrications about Ukraine that have been reported in the news.

I think the proof is in.

It's the Obama administration. And it's joined bipartisanly by most Washington politicians.

In the interest of transparency, I wish to admit that I voted for Obama twice. I contributed to his initial campaign, and in return received an invitation to his inauguration. I have no personal reason to denigrate him or to say things just to put him in a bad light. But I must say that there does not seem to be any flattering explanation for how the Obama administration has pursued its policies regarding Ukraine. Indeed, it's been shameful.

## What's the Agenda?

Why is the Obama administration trying to flimflam us about Ukraine? What's the motive?

I don't have any inside information about motivations. What I have learned, however, is that the reasons for America's involvement that have been given by the administration are not credible. I've provided representative examples attesting to that for you to see. There are lots more out there should you wish to do further research.

So the defense of democracy stories and the claims that America must stop Putin's march to conquer Eastern Europe are all demonstrably specious.

With those justifications now proved to be without merit, an obvious question stands out: Why is the United States involved? Why are Washington politicians of both parties united against Russia? Ukraine is not a strategically important country to the U.S. But the Obama administration is treating it like it is. Jack Matlock, Ronald Reagan's ambassador to the Soviet Union, recently commented: "how suddenly the territorial integrity of Ukraine or its independence has become a vital national interest of the United States is beyond me."

Yet inexplicably the Obama administration has taken a stance over Ukraine that outright confronts Russia and potentially threatens world stability. And since the confrontation is on a fabricated basis, it's hard to imagine a constructive way in which Russia can respond.

There have been far worse tragedies in the world than the violence that occurred on Maidan. Why then did the U.S. pick Ukraine as a cause celebre?

Is the U.S. involvement in Ukraine really about Ukraine? Maybe it is. Or perhaps Ukraine is merely an instrumentality for achieving some larger objective.

I'd like to relate three hypotheses I've heard,

each of which seems to fit the facts. That doesn't mean that they are necessarily true. But they fit the facts. I think they can be thought provoking and are worth considering as we await either confirmation or new explanations.

### #1 Dumb and Dumber

Someone once quipped that the reason for so much trouble in the world is because the politicians lie to the press and then believe what they read in the newspapers.

Quite a few American politicians have said some factually outlandish things in the press about Ukraine and Russia. I've quoted some of them in this book. I don't know for sure if the politicians believe what they've said, or if they are just pandering to audiences, perhaps in search of voters and campaign contributions. But their rhetoric has inserted a lot of unsupported and fallacious information into the news stream.

Then there are the false stories instigated by Putin's political enemies and others who have an ax to grind regarding Russia or Ukraine. I'm talking about stories like the Litvinenko poisoning, the Pussy Riot fiasco,

the Russia invades Georgia fabrication. If I
hadn't researched and analyzed these stories
myself, I might have fallen prey to their
misrepresentations, too.

Were the American politicians duped by all
those unsubstantiated stories? Do they really
believe that Putin is about to roll tanks
across Eastern Europe in search of
conquest? They've certainly acted as if they
believe it all. The U.S. has even moved
troops and military hardware into the region
in response to the alleged threat.

I've tended to doubt that any of the
administration and congressional people
could really be sincere in those espoused
beliefs. But maybe they really are? If true it
is quite an unbecoming reality that they are
so incurious and gullible.

This "Dumb and Dumber" explanation
nonetheless does fit the facts, though, to the
extent that we know them.

But so do a couple of other explanations.

## #2 Dr. Strangelove

When President Dwight Eisenhower left

office in 1961 he presented a farewell address to the nation. In it he warned Americans about the dangers implicit in the existence of a permanent defense industry. That's something worth considering as we search for a motive for creating the crisis in Ukraine. Here is the relevant excerpt from his address:

"Our military organization today bears little relation to that known by any of my predecessors in peacetime, or indeed by the fighting men of World War II or Korea.

"Until the latest of our world conflicts, the United States had no armaments industry. American makers of plowshares could, with time and as required, make swords as well. But now we can no longer risk emergency improvisation of national defense; we have been compelled to create a permanent armaments industry of vast proportions. Added to this, three and a half million men and women are directly engaged in the defense establishment. We annually spend on military security more than the net income of all United States corporations.

"This conjunction of an immense military establishment and a large arms industry is new in the American experience. The total influence -- economic, political, even spiritual -- is felt in every city, every State house, every office of the Federal government. We recognize the imperative need for this development. Yet we must not fail to comprehend its grave implications. Our toil, resources and livelihood are all involved; so is the very structure of our society.

"In the councils of government, we must guard against the acquisition of unwarranted influence, whether sought or unsought, by the military-industrial complex. The potential for the disastrous rise of misplaced power exists and will persist.

"We must never let the weight of this combination endanger our liberties or democratic processes. We should take nothing for granted. Only an alert and knowledgeable citizenry can compel the proper meshing of the huge industrial and military machinery of defense with our peaceful methods and goals, so that security and liberty may prosper together."

What's the relevance of Eisenhower's point? It is that a permanent defense industry, like any sector of an economy, will have self-interest in maintaining itself and indeed in growing.

And just as in a business sense umbrella makers might experience problems if climatic cycles brought on sustained droughts, those involved in the military-industrial complex would find a protracted relaxation of world tension to be problematic.

An economically threatened defense industry would wreak havoc over a large swath of the economy, well beyond the mere magnitude of government defense spending on record. It would threaten whole communities that are home to military installations and defense contractors. It would threaten consumer product companies that also have involvement in defense work. It would threaten those who have money invested in defense stocks. And it would threaten the campaign contributions to politicians from all the beneficiaries of a healthy defense sector.

In the lead-up to Maidan, the Obama administration was active in winding down military excursions in Iraq and Afghanistan.

It is not hard to understand how the defense industry, indeed, the military-industrial complex as a whole, might have felt a need to see the level of tension in the world tweaked a bit. That need could easily have been communicated to politicians via defense industry lobbyists.

There's one more fillip to the "Dr. Strangelove" hypothesis. It is entirely possible that a mid-2013 worsening crisis in Syria had been originally in the administration's crosshairs. Perhaps the administration had that crisis in mind to stimulate the defense sector. On August 24, 2013 *Slate* reported, "It seems likely that President Obama will bomb Syria sometime in the coming weeks." That surely could have raised world tensions and provided the defense sector a needed boost as Iraq and Afghanistan were fading from the picture. The expressed concern was that "Assad's forces have used chemical weapons, killing more than 1,000 civilians."

But before bombs began to fall, Putin inserted himself into things. On September 9, *Forbes* ran the headline: "Putin Offers Surprise Plan for International Control of Syrian Chemical Weapons -- Moves to Steal

Obama's Thunder?" The Putin plan succeeded in averting a U.S. bombing campaign in Syria.

While this may have been a political setback for Obama, it also was a financial setback for politicians in general. Just before Putin's surprise plan, Watchdog.org headlined, "Senators backing war in Syria are flush with defense industry cash." The story goes on to say, "it's not exactly new information, but the debate over Syria seems to have exposed -- once again -- the degree to which defense contractors and others stand to profit from the United States launching missiles at a foreign country." John McCain was tagged as a top dog beneficiary.

What does that have to do with Ukraine? It raises the question of what is the underlying motive for American intervention in Ukraine. Was the Ukrainian crisis stimulated in search of a replacement for the foiled plans for military action in Syria? Are politicians backing the American intervention in Ukraine "flush with defense industry cash"? The demand for campaign contributions seemed to be quite elevated in the 2014 election season.

An August 11, 2014 *Advertising Age* report supplies a calibration point for how ferocious the current demand is for political contributions. It says, "at this point in the last midterm election, in 2010, non-candidate and non-party groups had spent about $58 million to help elect or defeat candidates. The total spent by such groups by the beginning of August this year reached $152 million." That's some increase. And that's only part of the story. Ad spending not required to be reported to the Federal Election Commission, such as advocacy ads, would add to the total.

The Ukrainian crisis and the attendant vilification of Putin had perhaps an added benefit. It provided a payback to Putin for spoiling Obama's Syria plans.

So once again we have an explanation that fits the facts for the actions the U.S. government has taken with regard to Ukraine. This one would mean that Ukraine was no more than an incidental device with which to provoke tension with Russia.

## #3 Risky Business

In the classic 1967 movie, *The Graduate*, a

recent college graduate is taken aside at a party by an older gentleman wishing to offer advice. He starts, "Are you listening? One word: plastics." Then he adds, "There's a great future in plastics."

Today, in the context of the U.S.-Ukraine-Russia triangle, the one word is "gas." Natural gas.

In the United States, fracking technology and access to shale gas has greatly increased supply. In 2012 Associated Press reported, "So much natural gas is being produced that soon there may be nowhere left to put the country's swelling surplus."

In a market economy, excess supply of something leads to what's called a market surplus. When that occurs, it is typical that prices fall.

And the specific impact of the swelling surplus on gas prices? The U.S. Energy Information Administration reports that the cost of natural gas used in the manufacturing sector decreased by 36 percent from 2006 to 2010. That can't be good news for the gas business.

One solution for the embarrassing abundance of natural gas would be to export it. That would be possible technologically by liquefying the natural gas. Then it could be transported by ocean-going tankers.

Where would American producers ship their liquefied natural gas to? Europe is a large market. And according to the *Guardian*, Russia now supplies about 30 percent of Europe's natural gas.

Why would Europe want to buy natural gas from America instead of Russia? The choice might be influenced in America's favor if, say, Russia were to become regarded as an international outlaw.

Isn't that what we've been led to believe has happened as a result of the Ukrainian crisis? I.e., Russia is now an international outlaw. And one way the U.S. advocates punishing Russia for its alleged transgressions in Ukraine is to isolate it economically. In other words, don't buy its gas.

There's a seemingly large fly in that ointment, though. The facilities are not in place for liquefying and transporting American gas to Europe. It could take several years to get everything ready.

In a way, though, that is irrelevant. Time is not the only obstacle. There are legal hurdles to overcome, and there are objections from the environmental community. According to the Sierra Club, "Exporting natural gas would increase fracking and carbon emissions, put sensitive ecological areas at risk, and do nothing to address our country's energy challenges." The organization promises "to intervene in each and every proposed LNG facility across the country."

Those are serious obstacles. But would, say, a "crisis" help to expedite things and overcome the hurdles? Could saving our European allies from having to buy gas from an outcast Russia provide the impetus?

This all may be sounding like a covert plot too complex to be true. But there's no secret about it. On March 22, the *Washington Post* published an editorial titled, "Using U.S. natural gas as an energy wedge against Russia." That's the ticket to punishing Putin.

On June 25, *The Hill* reported, "House votes to speed up exports of natural gas." The story quotes Representative Cory Gardner saying,

"Allies around the world have told us that they would greatly benefit from American LNG."

With the force of this crisis to push through LNG, it all seems like a piece of cake. And the frosting on the cake is that all this action began early enough for politicians to have received generous campaign contributions from LNG interests in advance of the critical congressional elections of November 2014.

Risky business? What's the risk? This sounds like a clear winner for the LNG advocates and for the politicians. The downside only involves the Ukrainian people who have suffered through great upheaval in the crisis and the American environment that may be further despoiled.

## Adding Intent to Motive

The foregoing scenarios are possible explanations of motive. But is there any evidence of U.S. activities that revealed its intent to pursue those motives?

Earlier you saw how a State Department official was plotting the succession of power in Ukraine. And you saw how McCain was active in stirring up the Maidan crowd.

But throughout this saga there have been allegations of Russian interference in Ukrainian politics, too.

Often Putin has been accused of believing he has a right to influence developments in countries within Russia's neighborhood. That's usually presented as evidence of hegemonic intent.

Former ambassador Jack Matlock tried to explain Putin's mindset by drawing a comparison with America's Monroe Doctrine. Matlock said, "Americans, heritors of the Monroe Doctrine, should have understood that Russia would be hypersensitive to foreign-dominated military alliances approaching or touching its borders."

The Monroe Doctrine creates a justification for U.S. intervention in its own neighborhood. Specifically it's been used to explain American involvement in a variety of South American political situations.

So, Matlock underscores a powerful point. The Monroe Doctrine makes American policy toward Putin look like a do-as-I-say-not-as-I-do proposition. In other words it's okay for the United States to intervene when it claims to have interests at stake in other countries. But the U.S. doesn't consider it okay if Russia does the same.

Perhaps the Obama administration anticipated that possible criticism.

You see, just days before the commencement of Maidan, and with little fanfare, the Obama administration repudiated the Monroe Doctrine.

Secretary of State John Kerry said the doctrine "asserted our authority to step in and oppose the influence of European powers in Latin America. And throughout our nation's history, successive presidents have reinforced that doctrine and made a similar choice.

"Today, however, we have made a different choice. The era of the Monroe Doctrine is over."

The timing of this repudiation is very curious. Was it made with foreknowledge of impending events in Ukraine? Does it reveal an administration intention to avoid being characterized as duplicitous? Is this one more indication that the U.S. intended to precipitate crisis in Ukraine?

## So What's the Answer?

We've now seen three explanations for motives that fit the facts. We've also seen evidence of possible intent to stir things up and plan for the crisis.

But there's no smoking gun around to confirm any of the hypotheses.

They merely fit the facts.

But, you know, that distinguishes them from the explanations given by the Obama administration about Ukraine.

The administration's rhetoric on Ukraine does not comport with the facts.

Indeed, it's at odds with the truth.

# Chapter 11
# The Camouflaged Objective

*Is this the bottom line of it all?*

**WHEN** a journalist is sent out on an assignment, the first question he or she asks upon arriving at the scene is, "what's the story here?" In other words, what does the journalist see as the essence of what's going on.

Judging from the totality of the media reports on the Ukrainian crisis that I've seen, the essence of what journalists believe is going on is this:

"Putin, a power-hungry tyrant, has embarked upon the conquest of Eastern Europe to recreate the Soviet Union, and his first move has been into Ukraine. But he won't stop there."

Frankly, I don't know whether they are right or wrong. But I do know that they have failed to present any clear and factual evidence to back up the story. Instead, they've employed outright deception to make their case. You've seen that I've presented clear and factual evidence of that in this book.

Some readers might think this book affirms Putin's policy toward Ukraine. That would be a mistaken conclusion. I haven't addressed the merits of his policy. It is outside the scope of this book. Instead, I've merely pointed out how many of those who have attacked it did so through misrepresentations.

Where the truth lies on the policy is yet to be known. And it won't be known clearly as long as news sources continue to focus on fabrications instead of facts.

Other readers might see my criticism that Putin has neglected his international image as being overly harsh. It is intended to be harsh. As long as he allows his political enemies to control his reputation, he and Russia will continue to be branded in sweepingly negative terms, deservedly or not. And that will obscure any opportunity for a more reasonable and fact-based examination.

**What Have We Learned?**

Here are some of the takeaway points:

--Just weeks before Maidan, the Obama

administration repudiated the Monroe Doctrine that had justified past U.S. intrusions into countries in the Americas. At that time there was no apparent reason for the repudiation.

--A leaked secret phone call revealed U.S. State Department officials plotting regime change in Ukraine.

--Various U.S. officials publically promoted to the Ukrainian citizenry overly inflated expectations for a better standard of living through EU affiliation.

--American commentators actively reframed Ukraine's ethnic and linguistic diversity as amounting to points of division.

--Mass killings by sniper fire were blamed on Yanukovych, while authoritative suggestions that they were provocations organized by protestors are never conclusively investigated.

--An ensuing takeover in Kyiv by force and intimidation is characterized by the U.S. as a democratic transition.

--Legislators quickly tried to pass legislation

withdrawing official regional status of Russian language.

--In response Crimeans, in consort with Russia, moved to secede from Ukraine and reunite with Russia.

--U.S. takes an extremely strong stand against Russia's intrusion in Crimea, an American position that would have seemed duplicitous if the Monroe Doctrine were still intact.

--Civil war erupted in Eastern Ukraine when Kyiv forces attacked those who deny the legitimacy of the revolution.

-- U.S. attempts at substantiating direct Moscow military support for the Easterners are shown to have relied upon fabrications.

--A humanitarian crisis emerged when frightened Ukrainians fled to Russia from the war zone. The U.S. attempted a cover-up.

--In affixing overall blame for the Ukrainian crisis on Putin and Russia, the U.S. relies upon the psychological phenomenon of "confirmation bias" and on Putin's longstanding failure to actively protect his and Russia's reputation from malicious fabrications. A result is that observers are left without any definitive insights into what really happened and who is to blame.

--Various alternative explanations of the crisis fit the facts, but await substantial confirmation.

--Records of monetary contributions to American politicians suggest that the heightened world tensions stimulated by the Ukrainian crisis could have precipitated a beneficial windfall for the politicians.

## Late Developments

As this book goes to press, the revolutionary government in Kyiv on October 26 conducted a parliamentary election. It gave an overwhelming plurality to the parties of President Poroshenko and Prime Minister Yatsenyuk. With neither party achieving an absolute majority, a coalition will be needed to rule. We'll update you online when decisions have been reached. See Appendix I for details.

The parliamentary election is one of three elections that are now in dispute. First a

March 2014 resolution in Crimea favored reversion of the territory to Russia. And now is there is the parliamentary election.

The Crimean resolution was widely dismissed due to circumstances that surrounded it. On March 16 the White House said, "The international community will not recognize the results of a poll administered under threats of violence and intimidation."

But the October 26 parliamentary election was also conducted amidst alleged threats of violence and intimation, as reported by the *Kyiv Post*.

How did the White House respond to that?

Obama on October 27 called the parliamentary elections "a milestone in the democratic development of the country."

Why was one flawed election welcomed, and another rejected? Something's not right here.

The third disputed election took place on November 2 in Eastern Ukraine. It involved the areas around Donetsk and Luhansk. This region had never recognized the revolutionary junta that took over in Kyiv.

In May 2014 residents voted to constitute themselves as republics. The November election was merely to elect leaders.

But Poroshenko and the Obama administration seem to be using this occasion to further ratchet up the civil war.

Since this is all just breaking as we go to press, I will present a more detailed analysis on our update website. See Appendix I for details.

Meanwhile in closing, I wish to ask,

## What Hath the U.S. Wrought?

What have been the fruits that came of the U.S. and other foreign interests putting Ukraine in their crosshairs?

*Keep this in mind*: Before Maidan there were no fighting "separatists," the Ukrainian government was not killing thousands of its own citizens with military force, there was no civil war. Ukraine was whole. Sanctions were not causing ruinous economic damage to many countries. American-Russian relations were not in dangerous disarray. There were no war-torn Ukrainian cities, towns, and villages. Thousands of now-deceased Ukrainians were still alive. And the opportunity for replacing the unpopular leader Yanukovych through a democratic election was on the immediate horizon.

For the Ukrainian people and their quest for a better life, the effect of the foreign intervention has been an enormous disaster.

Their positive aspirations were used to manipulate them. The people were duped and exploited. And it all led to an unremitting crisis.

That's what the foreign intervention has wrought.

But Maidan, the revolution, and the civil war likely stimulated a windfall in financial contributions for American politicians to divvy up.

That's been some achievement, hasn't it!

# Appendix I
# Updates and Clarifications

UkrainianCrisis.Info is an adjunct to this book for providing updates. It will remain active until the end of 2015. (Use the case sensitive password: ukr599)

If information emerges that is pertinent to the points made in *Ukraine in the Crosshairs*, I'll post it there. The website is not intended to provide updates on developments in the news, however. Readers are encouraged to seek that information from active news organizations. Be mindful, however, of their propensities for distorting information as I've shown in this book. Apply the lessons you've learned here to news stories you subsequently see.

The website also serves as a repository for various photos or illustrations that are referred to in the book. You can access these images through the links that appear in the book.

New postings will likely be erratic. Readers who want to keep up on whatever new is posted are encouraged to avail themselves of the various free services available for providing alerts. A search on the term "detect website updates" will get you a list of possible service providers.

The website is intended neither to be a blog, nor a forum for discussion. However, I am interested in receiving substantive feedback from readers. Identification of any factual errors will be warmly received, as will be the identification of any pertinent points that might I have missed. I'd prefer not to engage in debates over points of view, however.

You may contact me at WilliamDunkerley@UkrainianCrisis.Info.

# Appendix II
# More on Language and Ethnicity

This Appendix expands upon the discussion of language and ethnicity initiated in Chapter 2:

The most recent Ukrainian census claims that the mother tongue for 68 percent of the population is Ukrainian. For 30 percent it's Russian. In addition, a phenomenon little mentioned in official circles is something called Surzhyk. It is a mishmash of Ukrainian and Russian that according to the Kyiv International Institute of Sociology is spoken by up to 18 percent of the population. It's sort of a Slavic Creole.

Some radicals claim they have been discriminated against because of language. But, OpenDemocracy.net presents relevant data: "According to research from 2007, less than 0.5 percent of Ukrainians felt discriminated against because of the language they speak."

That statistic is for the whole country, both Ukrainian and Russian speakers. As quoted in Chapter 2, Kramer alleges that there is discrimination of the Ukrainian-speaking majority. But the research shows that discrimination is close to zero. Kramer's assertion of discrimination does not appear to be supported by facts. Perhaps it is a political position intended to fuel divisiveness. The opposition to the use of Russian expressed by Kramer seems to be reflective of positions taken by a number of politicians from Western Ukraine.

## Stories Abound

Some Russian speakers are quick to describe past mistreatment they've experienced while visiting the West. I've heard a number of stories about that. For example, there was a person at a Shevchenko Square concert in Lviv. He told me he accidently bumped into another concert-goer and said "excuse me" in Russian. Thereupon he was subjected to so much verbal abuse for speaking Russian that he left quickly, fearing that the altercation might become physical.

Another story has a Russian speaker traveling by bus into Lviv from an outlying area. He was quietly conversing in Russian with another passenger. Upon overhearing that, an older man attempted to attack him, menacingly waving his cane in the air. Fortunately other passengers were on hand to subdue the attacker.

I suspect that not every Russian speaker has been subjected to that kind of treatment in Western Ukraine. But the specter of those sometime-incidents seems to be enough to make many Russian speakers circumspect about showing their cards in the West. And it just may inspire many Russian speakers to fear how they will be treated by the new government in the future.

So what we have here on one hand is a population that mostly is happy to relate to one another bilingually and with virtually no feelings of discrimination, and on the other hand political activists who want to suppress the use of the Russian language in what is in reality a de facto bilingual country. The anti-Russian rhetoric causes alarm with some Russian speakers who in turn press for official recognition of their language. That then arouses fears among Ukrainian speakers who fear that Russian may overtake Ukrainian.

## Revolutionaries Instill Fear

When the interim government moved to discontinue the official use of Russian regionally, it struck fear among Russian speakers. It is ironic that this language legislation never went into effect. But the precipitous legislative initiative seems to have instantly hit a nerve.

The *Tampa Bay Times* actually did some investigative reporting on the timeline. Here's the sequence of events the newspaper found:

"The parliament voted on Sunday, March 2 [to repeal the law that had permitted official use of Russian regionally]. By Wednesday, a backlash had begun, but not solely in Russian quarters. That day, the western city of Lviv, a center of Ukrainian nationalism, protested the repeal of the 2012 law and declared a day of speaking Russian. The government of Hungary slammed the move as well. By Friday, Russian troops had taken positions at the airports and other key centers in Crimea. On Sunday, the interim president Oleksandr Turchynov, stepped in and said he would not sign the repeal into law."

So it seems that the decision not to sign the divisive law was not the president's wise instant reaction to the content of the legislation, but rather a result of external pressure.

## Objectiveness

Along these lines, there are two surveys that help to illuminate the language picture.

First is a 2011 survey by the Razumkov Center. It found that that only 31.8 percent of Ukrainian citizens are proud of the Ukrainian language. The survey further disclosed that 53.3 percent use Ukrainian at home, 44.5 percent use Russian. Those figures change only slightly for language choice in public places: 49.2 percent use Ukrainian, 48.7 percent use Russian.

Second there is a Rating Group survey of 2012. The results there found that 45 percent of the population speaks Ukrainian at home, 39 percent Russian. Unlike the Razumkov study, this one asked about bilinguality. It found that 15 percent of respondents speak both Ukrainian and Russian at home equally.

The most recent Ukrainian census was conducted in 2001. Its results indicate that Russian is the mother tongue for less than one third of the population. But Nicolai Petro related a story about a nationwide Gallup poll that was taken in 2008. Pollsters offered participants the same survey in their choice of language. Petro said that "83 percent of Ukrainians preferred to take the survey in Russian, and only 17 percent in Ukrainian."

## Is the Message Clear?

The degree of mutual misunderstanding among language groups reminded me of my experience in Latvia back in 1994. I was there to counsel Latvian media managers on strategies and techniques that would help their businesses survive the economic transition their country was going through. I quickly learned of the bitterness many of them had toward Russians. It was so pointed that I didn't let on that I knew even a single word of Russian.

One person told me that in the Soviet period before Stalin's death, an uncle was seized, sent away, and never heard from again. Another explained that she was born in

Siberia because her parents had been sent there as political prisoners. These were sad stories told with great passion. The people considered Latvia's current Russian-speaking population to be remnants of a resented occupation.

On one evening away from my students, I heard the other side of the story while at a restaurant. I had asked the waitress how to say a certain phrase in Latvian. She told me, but was quick to point out that she was Russian, not Latvian. Then she opened up with her own sad story, told with great passion, too.

She explained that she had been born in Latvia and regarded it as her homeland. Her ethnically Russian mother had been born there too. Her sadness came from the fact that after the end of the Soviet Union, she and her mother were considered non-citizens under Latvian law in a land they considered their home.

They had been disenfranchised. She felt betrayed that in order to become citizens they would have to go through a naturalization process that included Latvian language and history exams.

Perhaps the specter of how Russian speakers were treated in the Baltics is now fueling the fears of Russian speakers in Ukraine as some believe that country seems to be narrowing its ethnic self-perception.

So here with Latvia was another example of grave mutual misunderstanding that has a language connection and is rooted in the past. Each side has an understandable point of view. But they both miss the big picture: the here-and-now benefits of coexistence, mutual respect, and getting along together.

## More Statistics

The Ukrainian census seems to have no provision for counting people of mixed ethnicity. That means a choice would be forced at census time, and someone who was Russian-Ukrainian would be counted only as one or the other. If you project that process back for several generations you can get an idea of how non-differentiating ethnic categorizations in Ukraine actually are.

A U.S. Bureau of Census report titled "Ethnic Reidentification in Ukraine," concludes that "many centuries of mixed marriages produced a heterogeneous population."

And the 20 percent figure on mixes only refers to Ukrainian-Russian mixes. On top of that are the Ukrainian mixes with other ethnicities that make up what was characterized as a population that is "widely intermixed."

The Ukrainian census question on ethnicity presumes that there are distinct, mutually exclusive categories. But in reality they do not seem to exist.

Mixed marriages are not the only factor that beclouds Ukraine's ethnic profile. A growing number of people are reidentifying themselves from Russian to Ukrainian. According to the U.S. Bureau of Census report, "In the last several years, a number of surveys indicate a growing share of the population identifying itself as Ukrainian while the Russian portion is decreasing. At the same time, a growing percentage of women register their children as Ukrainian. The Russian share, again, is decreasing proportionately. These factors point to an ongoing reidentification..."

So when the official census claims that Ukrainian citizens are 78 percent ethnically Ukrainian and 17 percent ethnically Russian, what does that actually mean? The terms are not so differentiating as the media reports would lead you to believe.

## And Language?

Things are similarly indistinct when it comes to language. Just over two-thirds of the people claim Ukrainian as their mother tongue. Just under one-third claim Russian. Ambiguity exists, though, because the term "mother tongue" is not carefully defined.

Furthermore there's the fact that the census statistics don't account for bilinguality. The 2012 Rating Group survey did cover bilinguality. It found 20 percent of respondents claim both Russian and Ukrainian as their mother tongue. Fifty percent claim just Ukrainian as their mother tongue, 29 percent Russian.

It's also worth noting that studies of language usage at home and in public do not correlate closely with the "mother tongue" reports.

There is confirmatory evidence in the Rating Group survey results. In a 2014 update it tracked opinions for-or-against adding

Russian as a second national state language. The general trend is that the number of people supporting official national status for Russian went from 52 percent in 2009 down to 34 percent in June 2014. Over that same period, those opposing national status for Russian went from 41 percent to 61 percent. There was a three year stretch in the middle during which people were almost evenly divided on the issue. Were these changes a result of increasing political rhetoric?

The survey also measured intensity of opinion. The results indicate that for both groups, i.e., pro or con, the intensity of their attitudes diminished over the period of the survey. At the start, 75 percent of the pro group and 80 percent of the anti group felt strongly.

The intensity drop was greatest for those who favor official national status for Russian. It dropped by 25 percentage points. In other words, many people lost their fervor for according official status nationally for Russian. The drop for the group in opposition fell by just 15 percent. That means those against giving status to Russian didn't lose as much steam as those favoring it.

The general attitudinal shift over five years from a majority favoring to a majority opposing is remarkable. It included some dramatic ups and downs along the way that certainly do not look like the effect of a natural evolution of views.

I asked the Rating Group to comment on this. A response came promptly from Oleksiy Antypovych, principal of the group. He told me he believes that emotional factors are responsible for the fluctuations. He says that under President Yushchenko the prevailing opinion was in support of Russian as a second state language. That continued during Yanukovych's presidential campaign when he promised to give official status to Russian. After Yanukovych was elected, people lost trust in his promises, Antypovych says, and things dropped to the 50:50 split that lasted for three years.

But the most dramatic shift came later when the 2014 revolution and civil war broke out. Antypovych reports that attitudes worsened toward Russia in general, and a record low was achieved in support of official national status for the Russian language.

## The Political Angle

The 2012 Rating Group survey also shows that the sentiment for denying state status to the Russian language is closely related to location (West) and political party (Svoboda, for instance).

The Svoboda party was the target of a 2012 official resolution of the European Parliament. It called Svoboda "racist, anti-Semitic, and xenophobic" and pointed out that its views "go against the EU's fundamental values and principles."

I don't know whether or not Svoboda was active in inciting antagonism over language issues. But what the EU resolution does tell us is that for some time there have been forces afoot in Ukraine that seek to polarize society.

# Appendix III
# Artillery or Grain Harvesters?

Chapter 7 discussed controversial satellite images that were distributed by NATO to support its contention that there have been active Russian military operations within Ukraine.

One of the NATO-distributed images claims to show a Russian artillery battery operating on Ukrainian soil. Whether or not it is Russian is one issue. But someone has alleged that the photos are actually of grain harvesting equipment.

The image in question can be seen at:
http://www.UkrainianCrisis.Info/110

I extracted a close-up of two of the artillery guns shown. It can be seen at:
http://www.UkrainianCrisis.Info/111

And for comparison, here is an image of grain harvesters in the American heartland:
http://www.UkrainianCrisis.Info/112

The original NATO image includes a group of objects identified as support vehicles. Here is a close-up:
http://www.UkrainianCrisis.Info/113
Note that the two objects on the left appear to be an artillery gun with its barrel extended over the top of a truck.

And for comparison, here is an image of a grain harvester with its boom extending over a truck as it off-loads its grain into the bed of the truck:
http://www.UkrainianCrisis.Info/114

I have expertise in neither artillery batteries nor grain harvesters. So I shared my photo comparisons with others and received feedback from two individuals in whom I have considerable confidence. The first is a person who is experienced in military matters and photo interpretation. He ruled out these photos being of grain harvesters because of the shapes. But he pointed out that the images appear to have been degraded. The other response came from someone whose experience includes satellite control of seeders and harvesters. He said the photos are not clear enough to say absolutely that the objects are grain harvesters. But he considers the case is strong enough: eighty percent probability, he asserts.

So while there was disagreement on the artillery vs. grain harvester question, there is agreement that the images are not clear.

Since these images purportedly came from a commercial supplier, I looked into the kind of resolution that is available from such sources. Here's what I've been able to glean from various sources:

Until the summer of 2014, the Department of Commerce limited commercial satellite images to 0.50 m resolution. Now it's been changed to allow 0.25. Digital Globe, NATO's commercial image supplier, said the change was effective immediately on June 6, 2014. At that time, its newest satellite had a resolution of 0.46 m, and an older one with less storage capability had a resolution of 0.41 m.

But on August 13, Digital Globe launched a new satellite that has 0.31 m resolution. The images distributed by NATO are dated after August 20. It is unclear whether Digital Globe was already selling images from their new satellite by that date.

Digital Globe's website contains a number of illustrative images that are shown for marketing purposes. One such is of cars in a parking lot. Here is a portion of that photo: http://www.UkrainianCrisis.Info/115

Compare that with the image showing support vehicles associated with the artillery battery: http://www.UkrainianCrisis.Info/113 The cars look sharper to me.

But now here is a segment from a different NATO-distributed photo depicting an alleged Russian military convoy within Ukraine: http://www.UkrainianCrisis.Info/116 It looks comparable to if not better than the cars in the parking lot.

I don't know why the artillery battery images are so much fuzzier than the others. Digital Globe still operates older satellites with resolutions of 0.82 m and 0.55 m. It's possible that the image came from one of them. Or, NATO could have degraded a higher resolution image of the artillery battery to the point that it can't clearly be differentiated from a grain harvester. I haven't seen any convincing evidence to conclude one way or another.

But NATO did assure me that the images they distributed are unchanged from what they received from Digital Globe. That is, if these really are Digital Globe images. Strangely, the company is unwilling to confirm that, even though the images have been widely distributed bearing the Digital Globe name and logo.

## Appendix IV
# About the Author

William Dunkerley is a media business analyst and consultant specializing in post-communist countries. He is a Senior Fellow at the American University in Moscow. He works extensively with media organizations in Eastern Europe and the former Soviet Union, and has advised government leaders on strategies for building press freedom and a healthy media sector.

Mr. Dunkerley has been a columnist for the Moscow Times, Komsomolskaya Pravda, and Sreda (Russia's first media management magazine), and has been published in other major newspapers in the region.

A featured speaker at media business conferences in seven post-communist countries, and at the World Congresses of the International Federation of Journalists and the World Association of Newspapers, Mr. Dunkerley has also appeared on national radio and TV in Eastern Europe and the former Soviet Union, and is a frequent media interview subject on topics concerning the region.

Mr. Dunkerley is the author of *The Phony Litvinenko Murder* (www.omnicompress.com/plm), a book that analyzes the sensational death of reputed spy Alexander Litvinenko and its attendant media coverage, and of *Medvedev's Media Affairs* (www.omnicompress.com/mma), focusing on Russia's media sector and its foibles.

He is principal of William Dunkerley Publishing Consultants, and editor and publisher of two industry publications: *Editors Only* (www.editorsonly.com) and the *STRAT Newsletter* (www.stratnewsletter.com).

## Omnicom Press

Omnicom Press, publisher of this book, was founded in 1981 to offer publishing products and printing services. It now offers print-on-demand books and e-books. The e-books can be read on PCs, laptops, notebooks, tablets, e-readers, and smartphones. (www.omnicompress.com)

www.ingramcontent.com/pod-product-compliance
Lightning Source LLC
Chambersburg PA
CBHW072122270326
41931CB00010B/1643